Sixth Workshop on Hybrid Approaches to Translation 2016 (HyTra 6)

Held at the 26th International Conference on Computational Linguistics (COLING 2016)

Osaka, Japan
11 December 2016

ISBN: 978-1-5108-3325-8

Preface

Welcome to the Sixth Workshop on Hybrid Approaches to Translation (HyTra-6) held in conjunction with COLING-2016 in Osaka!

The workshop series on Hybrid Approaches to Translation aims at providing a communication platform, building a research community and informing research agenda around theoretical and practical issues of Hybrid MT, and specifically the problems, methodologies, resources and theoretical ideas which originate outside the mainstream MT paradigm, but have potential to enhance the quality of state-of-the-art MT systems. The workshop series fills a gap in the current paradigm allowing researchers to explore new pathways of bringing together a diverse range of technologies, methods and tools into the MT domain.

The current Sixth Workshop on Hybrid Approaches to Translation builds on a successful series of past events held in conjunction with international conferences:

HyTra-1 was held (together with the ESIRMT workshop) as a joint 2-day workshop at EACL 2012, Avignon, France: http://www-lium.univ-lemans.fr/esirmt-hytra/

HyTra-2 took place as a full-day workshop and was co-located with ACL 2013 in Sophia, Bulgaria: http://hytra.barcelonamedia.org/hytra2013/

HyTra-3 was a 1-day workshop at EACL 2014 in Gothenburg, Sweden. This workshop for the first time included an Industry Session – with invited talks of representatives from several companies, such as BMMT, SDL, Systran, Tilde, Lingenio, who highlighted an emerging industrial uptake of the Hybrid MT field by major developers of industrial MT systems: http://parles.upf.edu/llocs/plambert/hytra/hytra2014/

With HyTra-4 being held at ACL 2016 in Beijing, the HyTra workshop series for the first time moved to Asia. This edition again hosted an industrial sesssion with representatives from Baidu, CCID TransTech and Lingenio: http://glicom.upf.edu/hytra2015/

The last edition of HyTra, namely HyTra-5, took place in Riga, Latvia, and was co-located with the 2016 edition of the Annual Meeting of the European Association for Machine Translation: http://glicom.upf.edu/hytra2016/

HyTra workshops have attracted a good number of submissions and participants each time, and included invited talks, full papers, and poster sessions. The invited speakers were Philipp Koehn (HyTra-1), Hermann Ney, Will Lewis and Chris Quirk (HyTra-2), Hans Uszkoreit and Joakim Nivre (HyTra-3), Hinrich Schütze and Gerard de Melo (HyTra-4) and Andy Way (HyTra-5). The range of topics covered addresses all the areas of linguistic analysis relevant to MT, such as morphology, syntax, discourse, named entity recognition, etc., and a range of underlying MT architectures – statistical and rule-based. The workshops allow sufficient time for panel discussions which take form of exploratory brainstorming sessions and address further pathways of the development and integration of the hybrid MT technologies.

For the HyTra-6 workshop we have accepted eight papers which appear in this volume. The workshop hosts an invited talk by Mark Seligman, CEO of Spoken Translation, Inc.

We hope HyTra-6 will become a successful continuation of the HyTra workshop series and will result in interesting discussions, ideas and collaborations.

Patrik Lambert, WebInterpret, Barcelona
Bogdan Babych, University of Leeds
Kurt Eberle, Lingenio GmbH, Heidelberg
Rafael E. Banchs, Institute for Infocomm Research, Singapore
Reinhard Rapp, University of Mainz and Magdeburg-Stendal University of Applied Sciences
Marta R. Costa-jussà, Universitat Politècnica de Catalunya, Barcelona

Invited Speaker

Mark Seligman, Spoken Translation, Inc.

Organisers

Patrik Lambert, WebInterpret, Barcelona
Bogdan Babych, University of Leeds
Kurt Eberle, Lingenio GmbH, Heidelberg
Rafael E. Banchs, Institute for Infocomm Research, Singapore
Reinhard Rapp, University of Mainz and Magdeburg-Stendal University of Applied Sciences
Marta R. Costa-jussà, Universitat Politècnica de Catalunya, Barcelona

Programme Committee

Bogdan Babych, University of Leeds, UK
Rafael E. Banchs, Institute for Infocomm Research, Singapore
Alexey Baytin, Yandex, Moscow, Russia
Pierrette Bouillon, ISSCO/TIM/ETI, University of Geneva, Switzerland
Marta R. Costa-jussa, Universitat Politècnica de Catalunya, Barcelona, Spain
Josep Maria Crego, Systran, Paris, France
Kurt Eberle, Lingenio GmbH, Heidelberg, Germany
Cristina España, Universitat Politècnica de Catalunya, Barcelona, Spain
Christian Federmann, Microsoft Research, Seattle, USA
José A. R. Fonollosa, Universitat Politècnica de Catalunya, Barcelona, Spain
Udo Kruschwitz, University of Essex, UK
Patrik Lambert, WebInterpret, Barcelona, Spain
Maite Melero, Pompeu Fabra University, Barcelona, Spain
Reinhard Rapp, University of Mainz and Magdeburg-Stendal University of Applied Sciences, Germany
Serge Sharoff, University of Leeds, UK
Grigori Sidorov, Instituto Politécnico Nacional, Mexico
George Tambouratzis, Institute for Language and Speech Processing, Athens, Greece
Jörg Tiedemann, University of Uppsala, Sweden

Table of Contents

Workshop Program

Sunday, December 11, 2016 – Afternoon Session

14:00–15:30   **Research Papers: Session 2**

14:00–14:30   *Predicting Translation Equivalents in Linked WordNets*
Krasimir Angelov and Gleb Lobanov

14:30–15:00   *Using Bilingual Segments in Generating Word-to-word Translations*
Kavitha Mahesh, Gabriel Pereira Lopes and Luís Gomes

15:00–15:30   *Combining fast_align with Hierarchical Sub-sentential Alignment for Better Word Alignments*
Hao Wang and Yves Lepage

15:30–16:00   **Coffee Break**

16:00–17:00   **Research Papers: Session 3**

16:00–16:30   *Improving word alignment for low resource languages using English monolingual SRL*
Meriem Beloucif, Markus Saers and Dekai Wu

16:30–17:00   *Image-Image Search for Comparable Corpora Construction*
Yu Hong, Liang Yao, Mengyi Liu, Tongtao Zhang, Wenxuan Zhou, Jianmin Yao and Heng Ji

17:00–17:10   **Concluding Remarks and Closing**

Combining **fast_align** with Hierarchical Sub-sentential Alignment for Better Word Alignments

Hao Wang
Graduate School of Information,
Production and Systems,
Waseda University
oko_ips@ruri.waseda.jp

Yves Lepage
Graduate School of Information,
Production and Systems,
Waseda University
yves.lepage@waseda.jp

Abstract

fast_align is a simple and fast word alignment tool which is widely used in state-of-the-art machine translation systems. It yields comparable results in the end-to-end translation experiments of various language pairs. However, fast_align does not perform as well as GIZA++ when applied to language pairs with distinct word orders, like English and Japanese. In this paper, given the lexical translation table output by fast_align, we propose to realign words using the hierarchical sub-sentential alignment approach. Experimental results show that simple additional processing improves the performance of word alignment, which is measured by counting alignment matches in comparison with fast_align. We also report the result of final machine translation in both English-Japanese and Japanese-English. We show our best system provided significant improvements over the baseline as measured by BLEU and RIBES.

1 Introduction

Since state-of-the-art machine translation systems start with word aligned data, the processing of word alignment plays a fundamental role in machine translation. A reliable and accurate word aligner is considered as an essential component in the various implementations of machine translation, e.g., word-based model (Brown et al., 1990), phrase-based model (Koehn et al., 2003), hierarchical phrase-based model (Chiang, 2005) and tree-to-tree model (Gildea, 2003; Zhang et al., 2007). In general, word alignment is prerequisite for extracting rules or sub-translations (word pairs, phrase pairs or partial tree templates) for translation.

The most widely used word aligner is GIZA++ (Och and Ney, 2000), which is based on *generative* models, like IBM models (Brown et al., 1993) and HMM-based model (Vogel et al., 1996), in which parameters are estimated using the Expectation-Maximization (EM) algorithm. This generative approach allows GIZA++ to automatically extract bilingual lexicon from parallel corpus without any annotated data. Besides, a variation of IBM model 2 was implemented as fast_align[1] (Dyer et al., 2013), which allows an effective alignment of words. There is no doubt that fast_align is almost the fastest word aligner, while keeping the quality of alignment, compared to the baseline using GIZA++[2] (Och and Ney, 2003), or MGIZA++[3] (Gao and Vogel, 2008).

However, Ding et al. (2015) demonstrated that fast_align does not outperform the baseline GIZA++, especially for the distantly related language pairs, like English-Japanese or Chinese-English. The reason may be explained by the fact that, given a source word, fast_align tends to limit the probable target translation and its alignment nearest as possible to the diagonal in the alignment matrix according to the overall word orders, which is the drawback of IBM-model 2 (Brown et al., 1993) and its variations, in terms of being insensitive to word orders. The word alignments output by fast_align

---

[1] https://github.com/clab/fast_align
[2] http://www.statmt.org/moses/giza/GIZA++.html
[3] http://www.cs.cmu.edu/~qing/giza/

Proceedings of the Sixth Workshop on Hybrid Approaches to Translation,
pages 1–7, Osaka, Japan, December 11, 2016.

are often more compact represented in alignment matrices. For the case of distinct language pairs, this strategy damages the quality of the final alignment result.

Since IBM Model is restriction of one-to-many (1-m) alignments, some multi-word units cannot be correctly aligned. It is necessary to train models in both directions, and merge the outcome of mono-directional alignments using some symmetrization methods, for example, *grow-diag-final-and* (Och and Ney, 2003). Though this method can overcome the mentioned deficiency to some degree, the strong assumption of 1-m alignment forces the aligner to generate 1-best alignments, which is prone to learn noisy rules due to alignment or segmentation mistakes. Another problem exists is that the production of 1-m alignment losses the structural information of the whole sentence while phrase-based (or other kinds of statistical machine translation systems) relies on the continuous translation fragments. It has been proved that by applying structural models such as Inversion Transduction Grammars (ITG) (Wu, 1997) will achieve some gain. ITG has been widely applied to word alignment, bilingual parsing, etc., due to its simplicity and effectiveness of modeling bilingual correspondence. However, inducing ITGs from parallel data would be time-consuming.

In this paper, in order to integrate ITG with IBM model, we propose to apply the hierarchical sub-sentential alignment (HSSA) (Lardilleux et al., 2012) approach to realign word alignments. HSSA is an online word alignment approach, which was first introduced as complementary to `Anymalign`[4]. When fed with the lexical weights output by `Anymalign`, it yields comparable results with baseline MGIZA++. In fact, an important advantage of this approach is that it can be combined with any other existing approach by reusing the lexical weights output by this other approach. We make use of the structure named soft alignment matrix (Liu et al., 2009) to represent the alignment distribution for a given sentence pair, which cells are weighted by the lexical weights output by `fast_align`. With the recursive binary segmentation processing in HSSA, we realign the sentence pairs top-down. We also present a simple but effective method to deal with error alignment points produced by this hybrid method, i.e., conflicting cells in soft alignment matrices.

In Section 2 and Section 3, the notion of soft alignment matrix and HSSA will be introduced. The hybrid combination architecture of our proposed method will be illustrated in Section 4. Experimental results and the analysis will be given in the following Section 4. Finally, Section 6 draws the conclusion and future work.

2 Soft Alignment Matrices

A sentence pair matrix can be interpreted as a contingency matrix for the source sentence f (length J) relatively to the target sentence e (length I). Formally, given a source sentence $f = f_1^J = f_1, \ldots, f_j, \ldots, f_J$ and a target sentence $e = e_1^I = e_1, \ldots, e_i, \ldots, e_I$, we define a soft link $l = (j, i)$ to exist if f_j and e_i are probable translation. Then, given the word positions (j, i) in a $J \times I$ soft alignment matrix, $\mathcal{M}(J, I)$, a score w for each cell $\mathcal{M}(i, j)$ is defnded as:

$$
w(j, i) = \begin{cases} \alpha & \text{if } l = \varepsilon \\ \sqrt{p(f_j|e_i) \times p(e_i|f_j)} & \text{otherwise} \end{cases}
\tag{1}
$$

where w measures the strength of the translation link[5] between any source and target pair of words (f_j, e_i), in our case, the score $w(f_j, e_i)$ is defined as the geometric mean of the bidirectional lexical translation probabilities. The symmetric alignment between word f_j and e_i is visualized as a greyed cell $\mathcal{M}(i, j)$ in this matrix (see Figure 1). For example, the word pair ("japanese", "日本") is definitely aligned, but ("ink", "日本") is definitely unaligned.

In fact, the resulting soft alignment matrix makes it possible to refine the final output of alignments and reduce alignment errors. Since sub-sentential alignment interests us more than single word-to-word alignment, we define a score for phrasal case. Differing to the defination of phrase translation probability

---

[4]`https://anymalign.limsi.fr/`
[5]To avoid problems linked with data sparsity, Laplace smoothing was used here to handle the unseen alignments, with assigned a very small smoothing parameter $\alpha = 10^{-7}$.

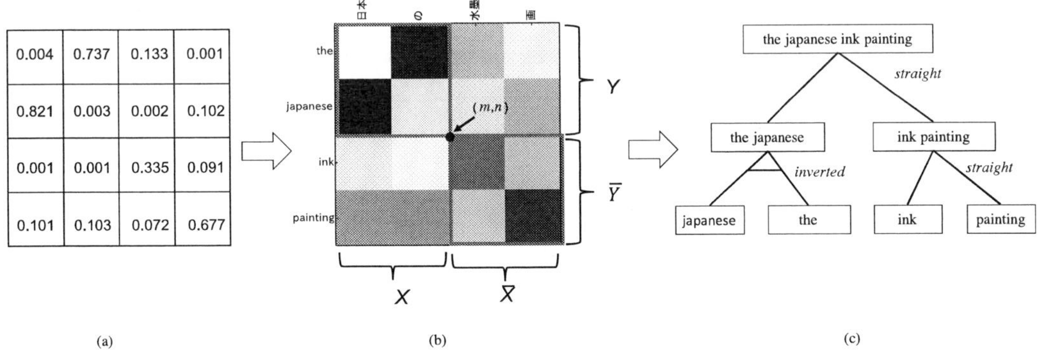

Figure 1: (a) A soft alignment matrix; (b) the grey-scale graph of soft alignment matrix; (c) corresponding ITG parsing tree. In Figure (a), cells are greyed from 0.0 (white) to 1.0 (black) on a logarithmic scale.

and lexical weighting (Koehn et al., 2003), the score of a block (X, Y) is defined as the summation w of the association scores between each source and target word pair inside this block as (Matusov et al., 2004; Lardilleux et al., 2012):

$$W(X, Y) = \sum_{f \in X} \sum_{e \in Y} w(f, e) \tag{2}$$

We employ the structure of summed area table for quick computation of the score $W(X, Y)$ in a $O(1)$ time complexity. Hereby, normalization of the probability distribution is not necessary. It should be emphasized that our soft matrix is estimated differing with the weighted matrix in (Liu et al., 2009).

3 Hierarchical Sub-sentential Alignment Approach

Given the soft alignment matrix, the HSSA approach takes all cells in the soft alignment matrix into consideration and seeks the precise criterion for a good partition in a similar way as image segmentation. HSSA makes use of an unsupervised clustering algorithm called *normalized cuts* (Shi and Malik, 2000), i.e., spectral clustering, or *Ncut* for short, to recursive segment the matrix into two parts. This procedure can be thought as being similar as the two rules in ITG: S (*straight*) and I (*inverted*). The ITG approach builds a synchronous parse tree for both source and target sentences, assuming that the trees have the same underlying structure (ITG tree) but that the ordering of constituents may differ in the two languages. In ITG, final derivations of sentence pairs correspond to alignments. A single non-terminal spanning a bitext cell with a source and target span corresponds to the final 1-to-many or many-to-1 HSSA alignment. In other words, HSSA performs the same kind of procedure as synchronous parsing under ITG. In ITG, there are three simple generation rules:

$$S : \gamma \to [X_1 X_2] \quad | \quad I : \gamma \to < X_1 X_2 > \quad | \quad T : \gamma \to w = (f, e) \tag{3}$$

During the segmenting, HSSA is supervised by the ITG constraint to decide the search scope of next level on the diagonal or anti-diagonal corresponding to the case of *straight* and *inverted*. HSSA terminates at the prerequisite condition when all words in source and target sentences are aligned and for each is a 1-1 alignment at least (corresponding to rule T). 1-1 means that one source word only has one aligned target word with strong confidence in both directions.

Consider a source phrase in Figure 1, $X\overline{X}$ split at index m corresponding to a target phrase $Y\overline{Y}$ split at index n. $Ncut$ is defined as (Zha et al., 2001):

$$Ncut(m, n, XY, \overline{XY}) = \frac{cut(X, Y)}{cut(X, Y) + 2 \times W(X, Y)} + \frac{cut(\overline{X}, \overline{Y})}{cut(\overline{X}, \overline{Y}) + 2 \times W(\overline{X}, \overline{Y})}$$

$$cut(X, Y) = W(X, \overline{Y}) + W(\overline{X}, Y) \tag{4}$$

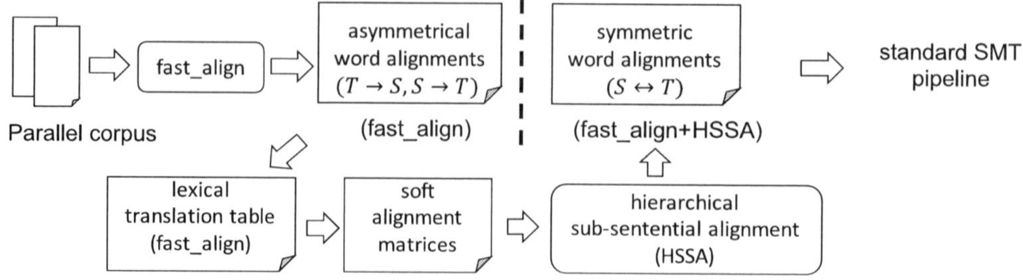

Figure 2: An example of our proposed hybrid combination architecture.

Each possible splitting point (m, n) in the matrix divides the parent matrix into 4 sub-matrices (XY, $X\overline{Y}$, $\overline{X}Y$, $\overline{X}\overline{Y}$). Either the two sub-matrices on the diagonal (XY, $\overline{X}\overline{Y}$) or the two sub-matrices on the anti-diagonal ($X\overline{Y}$, $\overline{X}Y$) will be chosen to limit the search scope on the next level. Hence, recursive segmentation eventually consists in determining the indices (m, n) which minimizes $Ncut(m,n,XY,\overline{X}\overline{Y})$ or $Ncut(m,n,\overline{X}Y,X\overline{Y})$ over all possible indices.

After computing the score of *Ncut*, HSSA decides for the next search scope (the upper left and lower right blocks in Figure 1) by finding the position where $Ncut(m,n,XY,\overline{X}\overline{Y})$ or $Ncut(m,n,\overline{X}Y,X\overline{Y})$ is the minimum value among all possible bipartite segmentation positions. In this example, $Ncut(m,n,XY,\overline{X}\overline{Y})$ is less than $Ncut(m,n,\overline{X}Y,X\overline{Y})$, equals to *straight* rule.

Since the time complexity of top-down HSSA algorithm is cubic ($O(I \times J \times \min(I, J))$, the worst case) in the length of the input sentence pair, it is faster than the original ITG approach $O(n^6)$ employing the CYK algorithm and achieves the same performance compared to (Zhang et al., 2008) which has a best time complexity of $O(n^3)$ with synchronous parsing.

4   Hybrid Combination Architecture

It is thus possible to use various word alignment tools, while `fast_align` provides the most effective pipeline with an acceptable time cost. Given the output alignments of `fast_align`, it is quite straightforward to estimate a maximum likelihood lexical translation table. We record both the direct $p(f|e)$ as well as the inverse $p(e|f)$ word translation probabilities in the translation table. This step is easy and fast finished with the `Moses`[6] training pipeline.

The purpose that drives us to do this work is the idea of combining two different models into one. One (ITG) models distinct language pair well, while the other one (IBM models) models similar language pair well. Previous work (Haghighi et al., 2009) proved that importing ITG limitations improves word alignments for Chinese-English alignment. An example illustrating our proposed hybridization is shown in Figure 2. In the context of system combination, we extend the pipeline of standard phrase-based statistical machine translation. In the middle, a soft alignment matrix (as the one in Figure 1) is generated for each sentence pair by feeding it with scores from the lexical translation table. On such soft alignment matrices, we apply the HSSA approach to obtain a final word-to-word alignment. Thanks to the simplicity of the HSSA approach, this can be done at no time cost (less than 1 minute in a real experiment on 320K sentence pairs). We employ the implementation *cutnalign*[7] for HSSA step.

Nevertheless, because HSSA outputs both 1-to-many and many-to-1 alignments, a drawback is, sometimes it returns some "noisy" alignments (referring to the alignment that appears weak in the soft alignment matrix). To solve this problem, instead of outputting all 1-to-1 matches contained in 1-to-many or many-to-1 blocks, it is better to prune low confidence matches while tweaking the alignments with heuristic search techniques, like the *grow* step in the *grow-diag-final-and* heuristic (Koehn et al., 2005). We consider that HSSA provides an alternative to *grow-diag-final-and* for alignments symmetrization in

---

[6] http://www.statmt.org/moses/
[7] https://github.com/wang-h/min-cutnalign

	#	MatchRef	Prec	Rec	AER	en-ja		ja-en	
						BLEU	RIBES	BLEU	RIBES
Ref	33,377								
GIZA++	31,342	18,641	59.48	55.85	42.39	**21.59**	68.10	**18.78**	65.87
fast_align	25,368	14,076	55.49	42.17	52.08	$20.79^{\ddagger}$	68.13	$18.23^{\dagger}$	65.25
+ HSSA 1-n/n-1	43,061	14,990	34.81	44.91	60.78	**21.23**	68.01	$\mathbf{18.14}^{\dagger}$	64.91
+ prune	27,982	13,542	48.40	40.57	55.86	**21.83**	68.42	**18.38**	65.53
+ grow	30,714	13,968	45.48	41.85	56.41	**21.53**	68.14	**18.53**	65.57

Table 1: Word alignment scores on English-Japanese and translation scores (BLEU and RIBES) in both directions (English-Japanese and Japanese-English). *prune* is the case when filtering all alignments in 1-n/n-1 blocks using a threshold $\gamma > 0.001$. Boldface indicates no significantly different with GIZA++ baseline ([†]: $p < 0.05$, [‡]: $p < 0.01$).

replacement of the intersection alignments of fast_align. Following this idea, we produce alignments with different strategy profiles.

5 Experiments

English-Japanese alignment and translation is a much harder task for fast_align than French-English alignment (Dyer et al., 2013). In our experiments, standard phrase-based statistical machine translation systems were built by using the Moses toolkit (Koehn et al., 2007), Minimum Error Rate Training (Och, 2003), and the KenLM language model (Heafield, 2011). The default training pipeline for phrase-based SMT is adopted with default *distortion-limit* 6. Two baseline systems, one built with GIZA++ and another built with fast_align, are prepared for result comparison. For the evaluation of machine translation quality, some standard automatic evaluation metrics have been used, like BLEU (Papineni et al., 2002) and RIBES (Isozaki et al., 2010) in all experiments. Since BLEU is insensitive to long-distance displacements of large sequences of words, we also use RIBES which was designed to take distinct word orders into consideration. In order to ensure a consistent, repeatable and reproducible experiment, we use the original training, tuning and test sets provided in KFTT corpus[8].

We first report the performance of various alignment profiles in terms of precision, recall and alignment error rate (AER) (Och and Ney, 2003) on the basis of human annotated alignment data provided with the KFTT corpus in Table 1. The first and second lines show the alignment difference using GIZA++ and fast_align. The original HSSA, which allows 1-to-many or many-to-1 alignments, outperforms the fast_align baseline from the point view of matching alignments and recall against the reference. The total number of alignments is much higher than with fast_align which victim of the "noisy alignments" problem mentioned in Section 4. AER and precision are behind fast_align, even more than GIZA++ baseline. However, (Fraser and Marcu, 2007; Ganchev et al., 2008) question the link between this word alignment quality metrics and translation results, like whether improvements in alignment quality metrics lead to improvements in phrase-based machine translation performance.

A lower AER does not imply a better translation accuracy. We show it in the following discussion. When sampling the alignment results, we found that the output of the proposed hybrid approach usually generates better alignments than the baseline.

Experimental results in both direction for English-Japanese and Japanese-English are shown in the right part of Table 1. Specially for Japanese, we skip the particles like {*ga, wo, ha*} and remove them from the data before implementing word alignments. Translation in both direction is improved significantly over the fast_align baseline[9] in BLEU and RIBES. It is not surprising that the pruning processing performs worse on Japanese-English not as well as English-Japanese, because a single English word may be aligned with several Japanese words. Perhaps deleting low confidence alignments in the many-to-1 case impacts consistency in phrases during phrase extraction. This is why *grow* slightly

---

[8] http://www.phontron.com/kftt/index.html
[9] On GIZA++ experiment, HSSA decreases in the final translation score somehow.

improved the final translation result.

6 Conclusion

This work presented a hybrid application of the hierarchical sub-sentential alignment approach with `fast_align`. It can be seen as an attempt to import the ITG framework into the IBM models. We showed that through the simple additional processing, our proposed approach yields better results than baselines. We also demonstrate that given reliable values, the heuristic alignment method based on word association (Moore, 2005) could yield competitive results with more complex parameter estimation approaches.

Acknowledgments

This work is supported in part by China Scholarship Council (CSC) under the CSC Grant No.201406890026. We also thank the anonymous reviewers for their insightful comments.

References

Peter F Brown, John Cocke, Stephen A Della Pietra, Vincent J Della Pietra, Fredrick Jelinek, John D Lafferty, Robert L Mercer, and Paul S Roossin. 1990. A statistical approach to machine translation. *Computational linguistics*, 16(2):79–85.

Peter F Brown, Vincent J Della Pietra, Stephen A Della Pietra, and Robert L Mercer. 1993. The mathematics of statistical machine translation: Parameter estimation. *Computational linguistics*, 19(2):263–311.

David Chiang. 2005. A hierarchical phrase-based model for statistical machine translation. In *Proceedings of the 43rd Annual Meeting on Association for Computational Linguistics*, pages 263–270. Association for Computational Linguistics.

Chenchen Ding, Masao Utiyama, and Eiichiro Sumita. 2015. Improving fast align by reordering. In *Proceedings of the 2015 Conference on Empirical Methods in Natural Language Processing, Lisbon, Portugal*. Citeseer.

Chris Dyer, Victor Chahuneau, and Noah A. Smith. 2013. A simple, fast, and effective reparameterization of ibm model 2. In *Proceedings of the 2013 Conference of the North American Chapter of the Association for Computational Linguistics: Human Language Technologies*, pages 644–648, Atlanta, Georgia, June. Association for Computational Linguistics.

Alexander Fraser and Daniel Marcu. 2007. Measuring word alignment quality for statistical machine translation. *Computational Linguistics*, 33(3).

Kuzman Ganchev, Joao V Graça, and Ben Taskar. 2008. Better alignments= better translations? *ACL-08: HLT*, page 986.

Qin Gao and Stephan Vogel. 2008. Parallel implementations of word alignment tool. In *Software Engineering, Testing, and Quality Assurance for Natural Language Processing*, pages 49–57. Association for Computational Linguistics.

Daniel Gildea. 2003. Loosely tree-based alignment for machine translation. In *Proceedings of the 41st Annual Meeting on Association for Computational Linguistics-Volume 1*, pages 80–87. Association for Computational Linguistics.

Aria Haghighi, John Blitzer, John DeNero, and Dan Klein. 2009. Better word alignments with supervised itg models. In *Proceedings of the Joint Conference of the 47th Annual Meeting of the ACL and the 4th International Joint Conference on Natural Language Processing of the AFNLP: Volume 2-Volume 2*, pages 923–931. Association for Computational Linguistics.

Kenneth Heafield. 2011. Kenlm: Faster and smaller language model queries. In *Proceedings of the Sixth Workshop on Statistical Machine Translation*, pages 187–197. Association for Computational Linguistics.

Hideki Isozaki, Tsutomu Hirao, Kevin Duh, Katsuhito Sudoh, and Hajime Tsukada. 2010. Automatic evaluation of translation quality for distant language pairs. In *Proceedings of the 2010 Conference on Empirical Methods in Natural Language Processing*, pages 944–952. Association for Computational Linguistics.

Philipp Koehn, Franz Josef Och, and Daniel Marcu. 2003. Statistical phrase-based translation. In *Proceedings of the 2003 Conference of the North American Chapter of the Association for Computational Linguistics on Human Language Technology-Volume 1*, pages 48–54. Association for Computational Linguistics.

Philipp Koehn, Amittai Axelrod, Alexandra Birch, Chris Callison-Burch, Miles Osborne, David Talbot, and Michael White. 2005. Edinburgh system description for the 2005 iwslt speech translation evaluation. In *IWSLT*, pages 68–75.

Philipp Koehn, Hieu Hoang, Alexandra Birch, Chris Callison-Burch, Marcello Federico, Nicola Bertoldi, Brooke Cowan, Wade Shen, Christine Moran, Richard Zens, et al. 2007. Moses: Open source toolkit for statistical machine translation. In *Proceedings of the 45th annual meeting of the ACL on interactive poster and demonstration sessions*, pages 177–180. Association for Computational Linguistics.

Adrien Lardilleux, François Yvon, and Yves Lepage. 2012. Hierarchical sub-sentential alignment with anymalign. In *16th annual conference of the European Association for Machine Translation (EAMT 2012)*, pages 279–286.

Yang Liu, Tian Xia, Xinyan Xiao, and Qun Liu. 2009. Weighted alignment matrices for statistical machine translation. In *Proceedings of the 2009 Conference on Empirical Methods in Natural Language Processing: Volume 2-Volume 2*, pages 1017–1026. Association for Computational Linguistics.

Evgeny Matusov, Richard Zens, and Hermann Ney. 2004. Symmetric word alignments for statistical machine translation. In *Proceedings of the 20th international conference on Computational Linguistics*, page 219. Association for Computational Linguistics.

Robert C Moore. 2005. Association-based bilingual word alignment. In *Proceedings of the ACL Workshop on Building and Using Parallel Texts*, pages 1–8. Association for Computational Linguistics.

Franz Josef Och and Hermann Ney. 2000. Giza++: Training of statistical translation models.

Franz Josef Och and Hermann Ney. 2003. A systematic comparison of various statistical alignment models. *Computational linguistics*, 29(1):19–51.

Franz Josef Och. 2003. Minimum error rate training in statistical machine translation. In *Proceedings of the 41st Annual Meeting on Association for Computational Linguistics-Volume 1*, pages 160–167. Association for Computational Linguistics.

Kishore Papineni, Salim Roukos, Todd Ward, and Wei-Jing Zhu. 2002. Bleu: a method for automatic evaluation of machine translation. In *Proceedings of the 40th annual meeting on association for computational linguistics*, pages 311–318. Association for Computational Linguistics.

Jianbo Shi and Jitendra Malik. 2000. Normalized cuts and image segmentation. *Pattern Analysis and Machine Intelligence, IEEE Transactions on*, 22(8):888–905.

Stephan Vogel, Hermann Ney, and Christoph Tillmann. 1996. Hmm-based word alignment in statistical translation. In *Proceedings of the 16th conference on Computational linguistics-Volume 2*, pages 836–841. Association for Computational Linguistics.

Dekai Wu. 1997. Stochastic inversion transduction grammars and bilingual parsing of parallel corpora. *Computational linguistics*, 23(3):377–403.

Hongyuan Zha, Xiaofeng He, Chris Ding, Horst Simon, and Ming Gu. 2001. Bipartite graph partitioning and data clustering. pages 25–32.

Min Zhang, Hongfei Jiang, AiTi Aw, Jun Sun, Sheng Li, and Chew Lim Tan. 2007. A tree-to-tree alignment-based model for statistical machine translation. *MT-Summit-07*, pages 535–542.

Hao Zhang, Chris Quirk, Robert C Moore, and Daniel Gildea. 2008. Bayesian learning of non-compositional phrases with synchronous parsing. In *ACL*, pages 97–105.

Neural Network Language Models for Candidate Scoring in Hybrid Multi-System Machine Translation

Matīss Rikters
University of Latvia,
19 Raina Blvd.,
Riga, Latvia
matiss@lielakeda.lv

Abstract

This paper presents the comparison of how using different neural network based language modelling tools for selecting the best candidate fragments affects the final output translation quality in a hybrid multi-system machine translation setup. Experiments were conducted by comparing perplexity and BLEU scores on common test cases using the same training data set. A 12-gram statistical language model was selected as a baseline to oppose three neural network based models of different characteristics. The models were integrated in a hybrid system that depends on the perplexity score of a sentence fragment to produce the best fitting translations. The results show a correlation between language model perplexity and BLEU scores as well as overall improvements in BLEU.

1   Introduction

Multi-system machine translation (MT) is a subset of hybrid MT where multiple MT systems are combined in a single system in order to boost the accuracy and fluency of the translations. It is also referred to as multi-engine MT, MT coupling or just MT system combination. Some recent open-source multi-system MT (MSMT) approaches tend to use statistical language models (LMs) for scoring and comparing candidate translations or translation fragments. It is understandable, because the statistical approaches have been dominant for the past decades. Whereas lately, neural networks (NNs) have been showing increasingly greater potential in modelling long distance dependencies in data when compared to state of the art statistical models. Therefore, the aim of this research is to utilise this potential in combining translations.

Since LMs are probability distributions over sequences of words, they are a great tool for estimating the relative likelihood of whether some sequence of words belongs to a certain language. Sentence perplexity – a probability score that can be generated by querying a LM – has been proven to correlate with human judgments close to the BLEU score (Papineni et al., 2002), that has become the main metric for scoring MT, and is a good evaluation method for MT without reference translations (Gamon, et al., 2005). It has been also used in other previous attempts of MSMT to score output from different MT engines as mentioned by Callison-Burch et al. (2001) and Akiba et al. (2002).

Most recently, different order LMs have been used in open-source MSMT approaches like ChunkMT (Rikters and Skadiņa, 2016). This system and the statistical model from KenLM (Heafield, 2011) that it uses will be treated as the baseline for further experiments.

This paper presents an enrichment of the existing MSMT tool with the addition of neural language models. The experiments described use multiple combinations of outputs from online MT sources. Ex-

Proceedings of the Sixth Workshop on Hybrid Approaches to Translation,
pages 8–15, Osaka, Japan, December 11, 2016.

periments described in this paper are performed for English-Latvian. Translating from and to other languages is supported, but it has some limitations as described in the original paper. The code of the developed system is freely available at GitHub[1].

The structure of this paper is as following: Section 2 summarizes related work. Section 3 describes the architecture of the baseline system. Section 4 outlines the LM toolkits that are used in the experiments and section 5 provides the experiment setup and results. Finally, conclusions and aims for further directions of work are summarized.

2 Related Work

Ahsan and Kolachina (2010) describe a way of combining SMT and RBMT systems in multiple setups where each one had input from the SMT system added in a different phase of the RBMT system.

Barrault (2010) describes a MT system combination method where he combines multiple confusion networks of 1-best hypotheses from MT systems into one lattice and uses a language model for decoding the lattice to generate the best hypothesis.

Mellebeek et al. (2006) introduced a hybrid MT system that utilised online MT engines for MSMT. Their system at first attempts to split sentences into smaller parts for easier translation by the means of syntactic analysis, then translate each part with each individual MT system while also providing some context, and finally recompose the output from the best scored translations of each part (they use three heuristics for selecting the best translation).

Freitag et al. (2015) use a combination of a confusion network and a neural network model. A feed-forward neural network is trained to improve upon the traditional binary voting model of the confusion network. This gives the confusion network the option to prefer other systems at different positions even in the same sentence.

3 System Architecture

The main workflow consists of three main constituents – 1) pre-processing of the source sentences, 2) the acquisition of translations and 3) post-processing - selection of the best-translated chunks and creation of MT output. A visualisation of the whole workflow is presented in Figure 1. It outlines the main constituents and sketches their internals.

Going into more detail on the chunking part of the pre-processing step, Figure 2 represents the basic workflow for that. The syntax tree of a sentence is traversed bottom-up, right to left and combines smaller subtrees with bigger ones when possible thereby creating chunks that are no longer than a quarter of tokens or words in the sentence. This specific maximum length for chunks was chosen in previous experiments that showed a general decrease of translation quality or no changes at all for longer maximum chunks. However, if the chunker returns a high amount of chunks for a single sentence, this maximum ratio can be adjusted further. More details on the chunking can be found in the paper of Rikters and Skadiņa (2016) and Rikters (2016).

For translation, several online MT systems are used. The paper of the baseline system described using *Google Translate[2], Bing Translator[3], Yandex Translate[4]* and *Hugo[5]*. Source languages require compliance with Berkeley Parser (Petrov et al., 2006) parse grammars. The parser is able to learn new grammars from treebanks. Target languages require a language model that is compliant with either KenLM or one of the NN LM tools. New LMs can also be trained using monolingual plain text files as input.

---

[1] Machine translation system combination using neural network language models - https://github.com/M4t1ss/Batch-ChunkCombiner
[2] Google Translate API - https://cloud.google.com/translate/
[3] Microsoft Translator Text API - https://www.microsoft.com/en-us/translator/translatorapi.aspx
[4] Yandex Translate API - https://tech.yandex.com/translate/
[5] Latvian public administration machine translation service API - http://hugo.lv/TranslationAPI

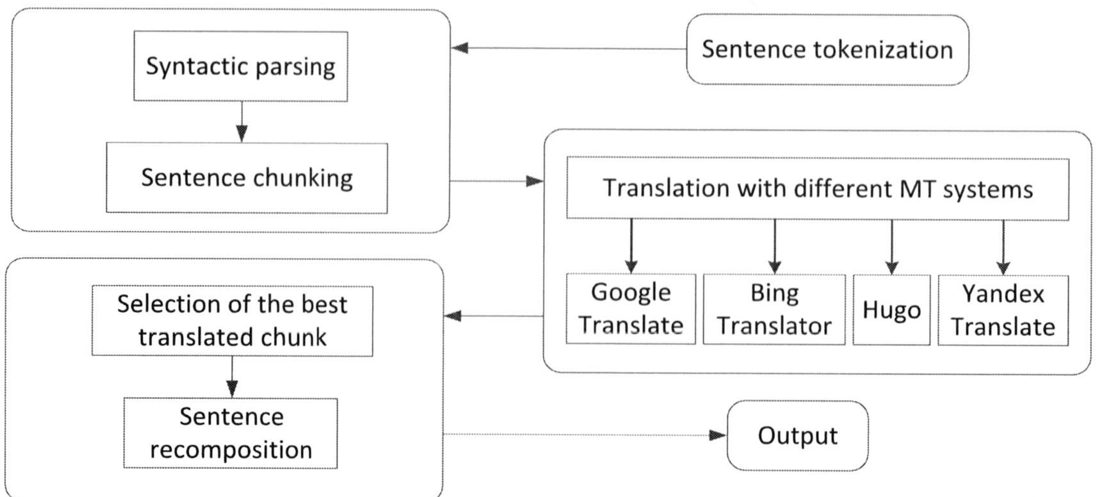

Figure 1. General workflow of the translation process. (Rikters and Skadiņa 2016)

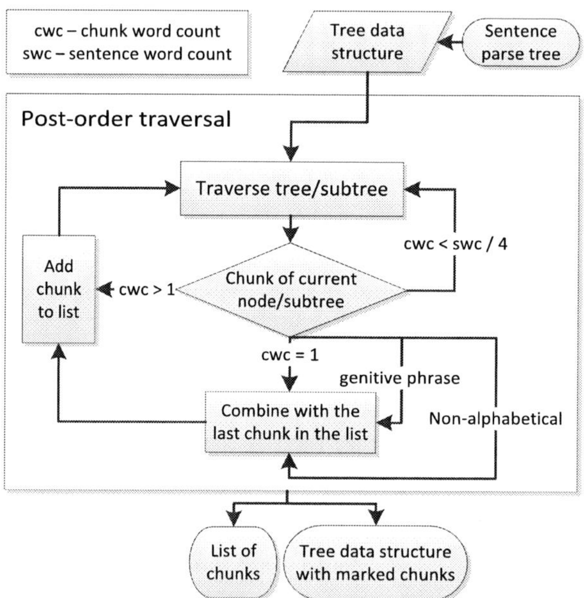

Figure 2. Illustration of how chunks are selected

4 Language Models

4.1 Baseline

The baseline language model was trained with the statistical LM toolkit – KenLM. It is an open-source tool for fast and scalable estimation, filtering, and querying of language models. It is one of the most popular LM tools and is integrated into many phrase-based MT systems like Moses (Koehn et al., 2007), cdec (Dyer et al., 2010), and Joshua (Li et al., 2009). It does the job quite efficiently, thus, it was included as the only LM option in the baseline system. For training, a large order of 12 was chosen for maximum quality.

4.2 RWTHLM

RWTHLM is a toolkit for training many different types of neural network language models (Sunder-meyer et al., 2014). It has support for feed-forward, recurrent and long short-term memory NNs. While training different NN configurations, the best results were achieved with a model consisting of one feed-forward input layer with a 3-word history, followed by one linear layer of 200 neurons with sigmoid activation function.

4.3 MemN2N

MemN2N trains an end-to-end memory network (Sainbayar et al., 2015) model for language modelling. It is a neural network with a recurrent attention model over a possibly large external memory with architecture of a memory network. Because it is trained end-to-end, the approach requires significantly less supervision during training.

MemN2N requires Torch[6] scientific computing framework to be installed for running. Torch is an open source machine learning library that provides a wide range of algorithms for deep learning. For training, the default configuration was used with an internal state dimension of 150, linear part of the state 75 and number of hops set to six.

4.4 Char-RNN

Char-RNN[7] is a multi-layer recurrent neural network for training character-level language models. It has support for recurrent NNs, long short-term memory (LSTM) and rated recurrent units.

To run Char-RNN on a CPU, a minimum installation of Torch is also required. Running on a GPU requires some additional Torch packages. The best scoring model was trained using 2 LSTM layers with 1,024 neurons each and the dropout parameter set to 0.5.

4.5 Environment

The translation experiments were carried out on Ubuntu server with 16GB RAM and 4 cores. This was sufficient because querying the models requires far less computation power than training.

Experiments for LM training and perplexity evaluation were done on three desktop workstation machines with different configurations. The KenLM and RWTHLM models were trained on an 8-core CPU with 16GB of RAM. For training MemN2N a GeForce Titan X (12GB memory, 3,072 CUDA cores) GPU with a 12-core CPU and 64GB RAM. The Char-RNN model was trained on a Radeon HD 7950 (3GB memory, 1,792 cores) GPU with an 8-core CPU and 16GB RAM.

5 Experiments

5.1 Data

To train the LMs the Latvian monolingual part of the DGT-TM (Steinberger et al., 2013) was used. It consists of 3.1 million legal domain sentences. In the case of training an LM with Char-RNN only the first half of this corpus (1.5 million sentences) was used in order to speed up the training process as well as because the character level model requires much less training data when compared with the others. When training all NN LMs evaluation and validation datasets were automatically derived from the training data with the proportion of 97% for training, 1.5% for validation and 1.5% for testing. The final evaluation data consisted of 1,134 sentences randomly selected out of a different legal domain corpus – the JRC Acquis corpus version 3.0 (Steinberger et al., 2006).

The translation experiments were conducted on the English – Latvian part of the JRC Acquis corpus from which both the test data and data for training of the language model were retrieved. The test data contained 1,581 randomly selected legal domain sentences.

For testing on a general domain, the ACCURAT balanced evaluation corpus (Skadiņš et al., 2010) was selected. The general domain test data consists of 512 sentences.

A 12-gram language model for the baseline was trained using KenLM.

---

⁶ A scientific computing framework for luajit - http://torch.ch
⁷ Multi-layer Recurrent Neural Networks (LSTM, GRU, RNN) for character-level language models in Torch
https://github.com/karpathy/char-rnn

5.2   Language Modelling Experiments

To justify using different language modelling approaches, different language models were trained with the same and similar (half of the corpus in one case) training data. Table 1 shows differences in perplexity evaluations that outline the superiority of NN LMs. It also shows that the statistical model is much faster to train on a CPU and that NN LMs train more efficiently on GPUs.

System	Perplexity	Training corpus size	Trained on	Training time	BLEU
KenLM	34.67	3.1M	CPU	1 hour	19.23
RWTHLM	136.47	3.1M	CPU	7 days	18.78
MemN2N	25.77	3.1M	GPU	4 days	18.81
Char-RNN	24.46	1.5M	GPU	2 days	19.53

Table 1. Results of language model perplexity experiments.

Since Char-RNN achieved the best results, several in-depth experiments were conducted using just this tool with varying training dataset sizes (for faster training) and NN layer combinations. Figure 3 shows how the network evolves in a setup with two 512-neuron layers. This experiment was conducted on a smaller dataset – only 1/6th of the corpus – allowing it to run for more epochs without early stopping. The perplexity on test data gradually decreased, reaching a lowest score of 22.18.

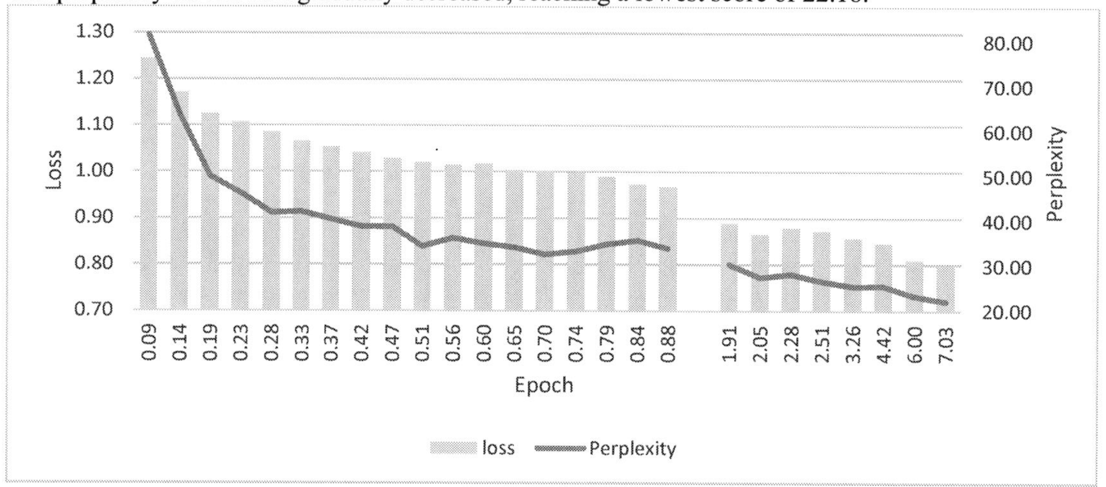

Figure 3. Changes of training loss and perplexity when training a two-layer Char-RNN with 512 neurons on 500 000 sentences.

Another variation for training a LM with Char-RNN is shown in Figure 4. Here 1/3rd of the corpus was used to train a 3-layer RNN with 1,024 neurons per layer. The lowest achieved perplexity was 21.23 after training one day on a GPU.

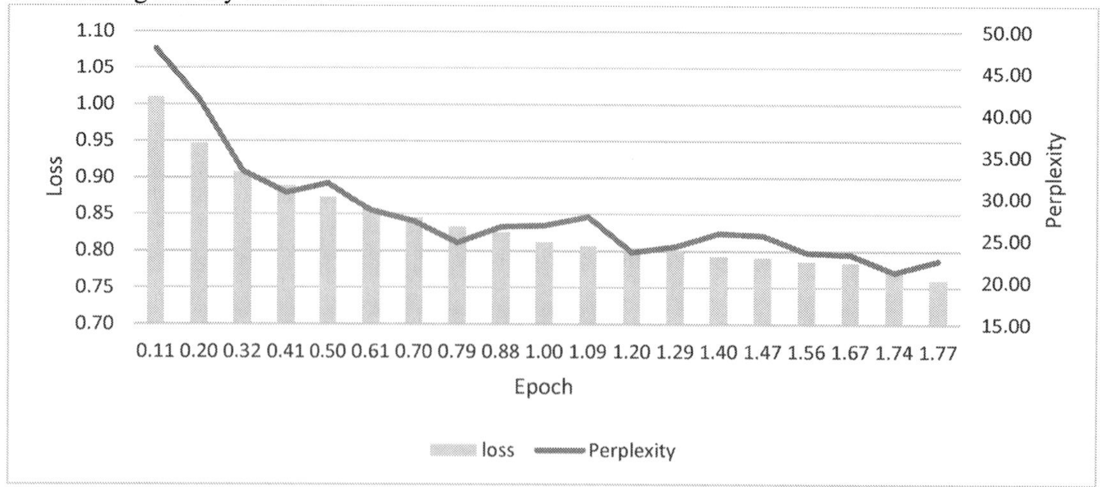

Figure 4. Changes of training loss and perplexity when training a three-layer Char-RNN with 1024 neurons on 1 million sentences

5.3   Machine Translation Experiments

The last column of Table 1 shows differences in BLEU scores when NN LMs were used. Correlation between LM perplexity and the resulting BLEU score is visible as well as a slight improvement in the overall result. Again, due to the outstanding scores of Char-RNN models, they were inspected closer to see how BLEU changes along with perplexity.

The following charts show how perplexity correlates with BLEU in translation test cases on the general domain and legal domain test datasets. Figure 5 represents results from evaluating a combination of Google and Bing (BG) online MT translations (denoted with darker blue colours) and a combination of Hugo and Yandex (HY) online MT (brighter blue colours) on the general domain test dataset. The trend lines (dotted) indicate that for this dataset the combination of BG stays mostly stable but the combination of HY gradually improves as the perplexity of the LM gets lower.

Whereas Figure 6 shows results of combining the same MT on the legal domain test dataset. In this case, while perplexity becomes lower at each time step, the linear trend line for BLEU score of the BG hybrid system does not show a tendency towards climbing higher. As opposed to the BLEU score trend line for HY hybrid system, that showcases improvement along with perplexity.

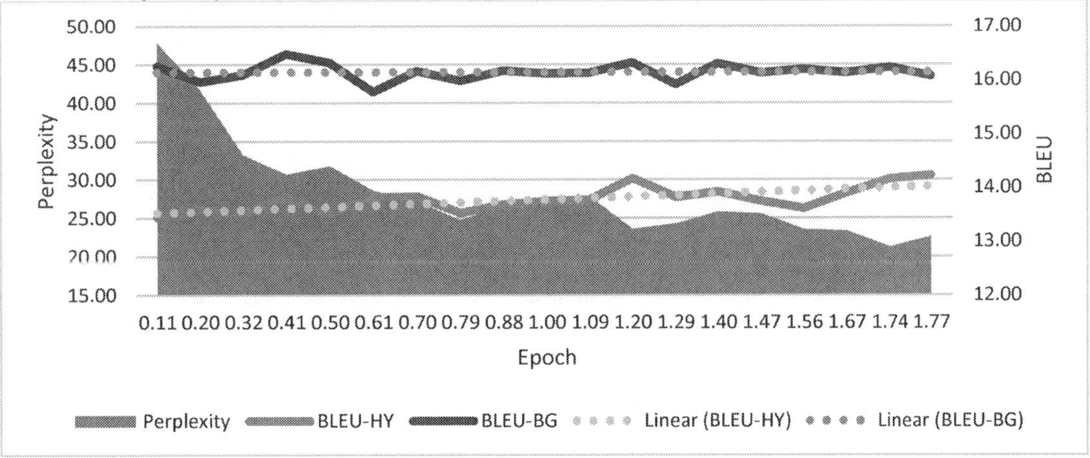

Figure 5. Changes of perplexity when training a three-layer Char-RNN with 1,024 neurons on 1 million sentences and its effect on BLEU score when used in MSMT for combining Bing and Google (BG); Hugo and Yandex (HY) on the general domain test dataset.

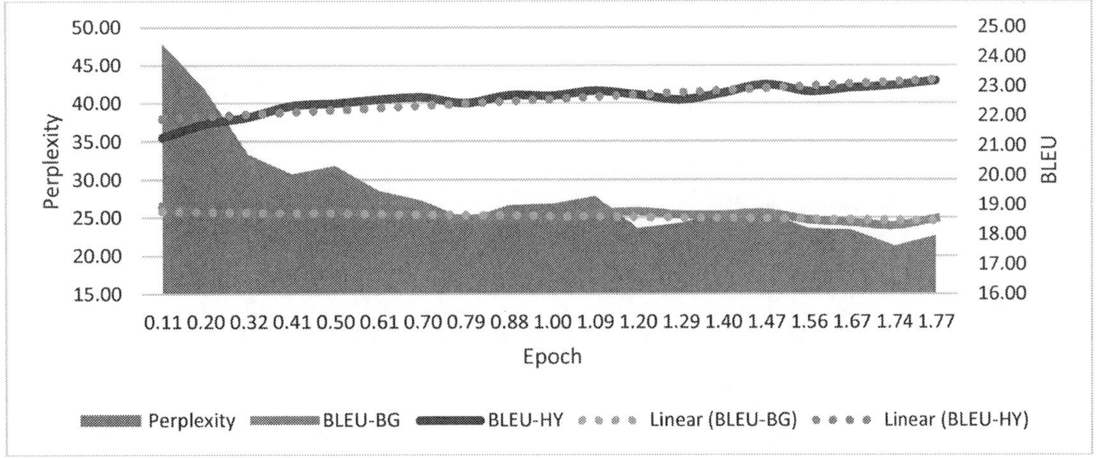

Figure 6. Changes of perplexity when training a three-layer Char-RNN with 1,024 neurons on 1 million sentences and its effect on BLEU score when used in MSMT for combining Bing and Google (BG); Hugo and Yandex (HY) on the legal domain test dataset.

Conclusion

This paper described ways to improve the baseline MSMT system with neural network language models. The main goals were to provide more options for language modelling in the translation combination tool and to improve translation quality over the baseline. Test cases showed an improvement in BLEU score, when used only with Google and Bing, of 0.35 BLEU points.

In the detailed translation experiments where a BLEU score was obtained in every stage of the LM training there was only a steady correlation of BLEU and perplexity in the case of using Hugo and Yandex translations, which were very different ($0.52 - 1.10$ BLEU difference with each other) to begin with. In the case of combining Google and Bing translations where the difference was far less significant ($0.3 - 0.8$ BLEU difference with each other), the BLEU scores of the NN model hybrid were less uniform with perplexity. This indicates that out of very similar options, even the NN model fluctuates with its predictions but it does get more confident in cases where the difference is more obvious.

Adding alternative resources to select from in each step of the translation process could benefit the more advanced user base. For instance, the addition of more online translation APIs like Baidu Translate (Zhongjun, 2015) would expand the variety of choices for translations. A configurable usage of different syntactic parsers like SyntaxNet - Neural Models of Syntax (Andor et al., 2016) is likely to improve the translation process.

Another interesting direction to investigate would be how this system performs when given translations of chunks from locally trained (instead of online) MT systems. For instance, a combination a Moses system with Apertium (Forcada et al., 2011) and even a neural MT system like Nematus (Sennrich et al., 2016).

Reference

Ahsan, A., Kolachina, P.: Coupling Statistical Machine Translation with Rule-based Transfer and Generation, AMTA-The Ninth Conference of the Association for Machine Translation in the Americas. Denver, Colorado (2010)

Akiba, Y., Watanabe, T., Sumita, E.: Using language and translation models to select the best among outputs from multiple MT systems. Proceedings of the 19th international conference on Computational Linguistics-Volume 1. Association for Computational Linguistics. (2002)

Andor, D., Alberti, C., Weiss, D., Severyn, A., Presta, A., Ganchev, K., Collins, M.: Globally normalized transition-based neural networks. arXiv preprint arXiv:1603.06042 (2016)

Barrault, L.: MANY: Open source machine translation system combination. The Prague Bulletin of Mathematical Linguistics 93: 147-155. (2010)

Callison-Burch, C., Flournoy, R. S.: A program for automatically selecting the best output from multiple machine translation engines. Proceedings of the Machine Translation Summit VIII. (2001)

Dyer, C., Weese, J., Setiawan, H., Lopez, A., Ture, F., Eidelman, V., Ganitkevitch, J., Blunsom, P., Resnik, P.: cdec: A decoder, alignment, and learning framework for finite-state and context-free translation models. Proceedings of the ACL 2010 System Demonstrations. Association for Computational Linguistics, (2010)

Forcada, M.L., Ginestí-Rosell, M., Nordfalk, J., O'Regan, J., Ortiz-Rojas, S., Pérez-Ortiz, J.A., Sánchez-Martínez, F., Ramírez-Sánchez, G. and Tyers, F.M., 2011. Apertium: a free/open-source platform for rule-based machine translation. Machine translation, 25(2), pp.127-144.

Freitag, M., Peter, J., Peitz, S., Feng, M., Ney, H.: Local System Voting Feature for Machine Translation System Combination. In EMNLP 2015 Tenth Workshop on Statistical Machine Translation (WMT 2015), pages 467-–476, Lisbon, Portugal. (2015)

Gamon, M., Aue, A., Smets, M.: Sentence-level MT evaluation without reference translations: Beyond language modeling. Proceedings of EAMT. (2005)

Heafield, K.: KenLM: Faster and smaller language model queries. Proceedings of the Sixth Workshop on Statistical Machine Translation. Association for Computational Linguistics. (2011)

Koehn, P., Hoang, H., Birch, A., Callison-Burch, C., Federico, M., Bertoldi, N., Cowan, B., Shen, W., Moran, C., Zens, R., Dyer, C.: Moses: Open source toolkit for statistical machine translation. Proceedings of the 45th annual meeting of the ACL on interactive poster and demonstration sessions. Association for Computational Linguistics, (2007)

Li, Z., Callison-Burch, C., Dyer, C., Ganitkevitch, J., Khudanpur, S., Schwartz, L., Thornton, W.N., Weese, J., Zaidan, O.F.: Joshua: An open source toolkit for parsing-based machine translation. Proceedings of the Fourth Workshop on Statistical Machine Translation. Association for Computational Linguistics, (2009)

Mellebeek, B., Owczarzak, K., Van Genabith, J., Way, A.: Multi-engine machine translation by recursive sentence decomposition. Proceedings of the 7th Conference of the Association for Machine Translation in the Americas, 110-118. (2006)

Papineni, K., Roukos, S., Ward, T., Zhu, W. J.: BLEU: a method for automatic evaluation of machine translation. Proceedings of the 40th annual meeting on association for computational linguistics. Association for Computational Linguistics. (2002)

Petrov, S., Barrett, L., Thibaux, R., Klein, D.: Learning accurate, compact, and interpretable tree annotation. Proceedings of the 21st International Conference on Computational Linguistics and the 44th annual meeting of the Association for Computational Linguistics. Association for Computational Linguistics. (2006)

Rikters, M.: K-Translate-Interactive Multi-system Machine Translation. International Baltic Conference on Databases and Information Systems. Springer International Publishing (2016)

Rikters, M., Skadiņa, I.: Combining machine translated sentence chunks from multiple MT systems. *CICLing 2016*. (2016)

Sainbayar, S., Weston, J., Fergus, R.: End-to-end memory networks. Advances in neural information processing systems. (2015)

Sennrich, R., Haddow, B. and Birch, A., 2016. Edinburgh Neural Machine Translation Systems for WMT 16. arXiv preprint arXiv:1606.02891. (2016)

Skadiņš, R., Goba, K., Šics, V.: Improving SMT for Baltic Languages with Factored Models. Proceedings of the Fourth International Conference Baltic HLT 2010, Frontiers in Artificial Intelligence and Applications, Vol. 2192., 125-132. (2010)

Steinberger, R., Eisele, A., Klocek, S., Pilos, S., Schlüter, P.: Dgt-tm: A freely available translation memory in 22 languages. arXiv preprint arXiv:1309.5226. (2013)

Steinberger, R., Pouliquen, B., Widiger, A., Ignat, C., Erjavec, T., Tufis, D., Varga, D.: The JRC-Acquis: A multilingual aligned parallel corpus with 20+ languages. arXiv preprint cs/0609058. (2006)

Sundermeyer, M., Schlüter, R., Ney, H.: rwthlm-the RWTH aachen university neural network language modeling toolkit. INTERSPEECH. (2014)

Zhongjun, H. E.: Baidu Translate: Research and Products. ACL-IJCNLP 2015 (2015): 61.

Image-Image Search for Comparable Corpora Construction

Yu Hong[✉][†] Liang Yao[†] Mengyi Liu[†] Tongtao Zhang[‡] Wenxuan Zhou[†] Jianmin Yao[†] Heng Ji[‡]

[†]School of Computer Science & Technology, Soochow University, China
{tianxianer, liangysky, mengyiliu22,chrisnotkris7}@gmail.com, jyao@suda.edu.cn
[‡]Rensselaer Polytechnic Institute, NY, USA
{zhangt13, jih}@rpi.edu

Abstract

We present a novel method of comparable corpora construction. Unlike the traditional methods which heavily rely on linguistic features, our method only takes image similarity into consideration. We use an image-image search engine to obtain similar images, together with the captions in source language and target language. On the basis, we utilize captions of similar images to construct sentence-level bilingual corpora. Experiments on 10,371 target captions show that our method achieves a precision of 0.85 in the top search results.

1   Introduction

We limit our discussion to the sentence-level comparable corpora. Each sample in the dataset is a pair of bilingual sentences whose constituents are translations of each other, mostly or in whole. Briefly, they contain semantically similar contents, although they are expressed in different languages. In order to make it easier to read, we name such a sample as a bilingual sentence pair. See an English-Chinese case as below (English translations are attached behind).

1) *UN Secretary-General Ban Ki-moon appointed "Red" from the Angry Birds as Honorary Ambassador for Green.*

2) *联合国秘书长潘基文   任命   "愤怒的小鸟"   中的   红色   小鸟   为   绿色荣誉大使.*
   United Nations   appoint   angry bird   from   red   bird   as   Honorary   Ambassador
   Secretary-General
   Ban Ki-moon
   for green culture

Large-scale comparable corpora generally contain rich and diverse bilingual translation examples, such as phrase-level equivalents as well as aligned words. Therefore, so far, such corpora have been admitted to be extremely useful in training translation models. During the past decades, great effort has been made by researchers (Rauf et al 2009, Skadina et al 2012, Santanu et al 2014 and Ann et al 2014) to construct and expand the corpora. They fulfilled the goal mainly by using cross-language content similarity measurement techniques. Lexical information, topic model, knowledge base and domain-specific terminology have all been proven to be effective in the acquisition of document-level equivalents (Talvensaari et al 2007, Li et al 2010, Zhu et al 2013 and Hashemi et al 2014).

Figure 1: Similar images and their captions in English and Chinese news websites (In this case, we would like to believe that an English journalist and a Chinese peer both attended the ceremony and took the photos from different perspectives, and then released them in the domestic news stories)

Proceedings of the Sixth Workshop on Hybrid Approaches to Translation,
pages 16–25, Osaka, Japan, December 11, 2016.

Different from the previous work, we employ similar images as the bridge to retrieve the bilingual sentence pairs. We suppose that captions generally represent the semantic contents of images, so that if two images are visually similar, their captions are very likely to be semantically comparable. Figure 1 shows two real images which are respectively crawled from the English and Chinese news websites. Listed below the images are the captions which, as usual in the websites, are written in the native languages (Note that the captions have been exhibited in (1) and (2)). Not just the similar images, it can be found that the captions are comparable as well.

Accordingly, we collect the captions of similar images from websites, and specify them as the candidates of bilingual sentence pairs. We rank the candidates in the order of image similarity, and determine the most highly ranked ones as the reliable bilingual sentence pairs. In practice, we build an image-image search engine. The engine uses images as queries, and retrieves similar images based on consistency of image features of scale-invariant keypoints.

In this paper, we aim to independently evaluate the proposed method rather than a well-structured sophisticated system, and answer the question of whether it is possible to capture the bilingual `cap-tion pairs` (sentence pairs) by image-image search, if they really exist. In reality, the system should additionally consist of the modules like crawling, webpage structure analysis and image indexing. For these modules, we only provide a brief introduction. Nevertheless, it is noteworthy that these techniques are undoubtedly important for mining large-scale comparable data from websites.

The rest of the paper is structured as follows. Section 2 overviews the related work. We present the methodology and detail the image-image search engine in section 3. Section 4 shows the experimental settings and results. We conclude the paper in Section 5.

2   Related Work

There has been a considerable amount of work done in acquiring bilingual comparable corpora. One of the most widely used methods is the bilingual dictionary based text retrieval approach. Talvensaari et al (2007) created Swedish-English comparable corpora based on Cross-Language Information Retrieval (CLIR). They extracted keywords from the documents in the source language, and translated them into the target language by using a bilingual dictionary. The translations were used as the query words to retrieve the document-level equivalents in the target language. Bo et al (2010) implemented a bidirectional CLIR by using English-French dictionary.

Su et al (2012) employed the Microsoft `Bing` Translator to produce pseudo equivalents. Their experiments show that the slightly weak translations can be used to construct comparable corpora. It was also illustrated that the performance of Statistical Machine Translation (SMT) trained on such corpora was better than using lexicon. Su et al (2012)'s work shows the possibility to utilize the pseudo equivalents and the boosting approach to iteratively improve SMT.

The recent work seeks to use topic model to improve CLIR. The key issue which is mainly considered in this case is to precisely calculate the similarity between the translations and the documents in the target language. Preiss et al (2012) transformed the topic models in the source language to the target language, and measured the similarity at the level of topic. Zhu et al (2013) utilized the bilingual LDA model and structural information in similarity measurement.

Besides, knowledge base like Wikipedia has been proven to be useful for the discovery of bilingual equivalents (Ni et al., 2009, Smith et al., 2010). Otero et al (2010) used Wikipedia categories as the restriction to detect the equivalents within small-scale reliable candidates. Skadinaa et al (2012) proposed a method to merge the comparable corpora respectively obtained from news stories, Wikipedia articles and domain-specific documents.

3   Methodology

First of all, we present the methodological framework. Then we introduce the crucial part of the image-image search engine, i.e., SIFT based image similarity measurement. Finally, we list the preprocessing methods for collecting and processing raw data.

3.1   Cross-Media Information Retrieval

Our method can be regarded as a kind of Cross-Media Information Retrieval (CMIR) technique. The main framework of CMIR is closely similar to that of CLIR. The only difference between them is the bridge used to link a text in the source language with the equivalents in the target language. For the former, the bridge is the image, while the latter the language (e.g., keyword and translation).

Figure 2 shows the framework of CMIR. We also provide that of CLIR for comparison. For our method, i.e., CMIR, we collect the texts which summarize the main contents in images, and map the texts to the images in a one-to-one way. On the basis, we search comparable texts by pair-wise image similarity measurement. By contrast, CLIR generally employs a slightly weak translator or bilingual dictionary to generate rough or partial translations (see Section 2). Such translations are used as queries by a text search engine to acquire higher-level equivalents, such as Talvensaari et al (2007) and Bo et al (2010)'s work, using the translations of keywords as the clues to detect document-level equivalents.

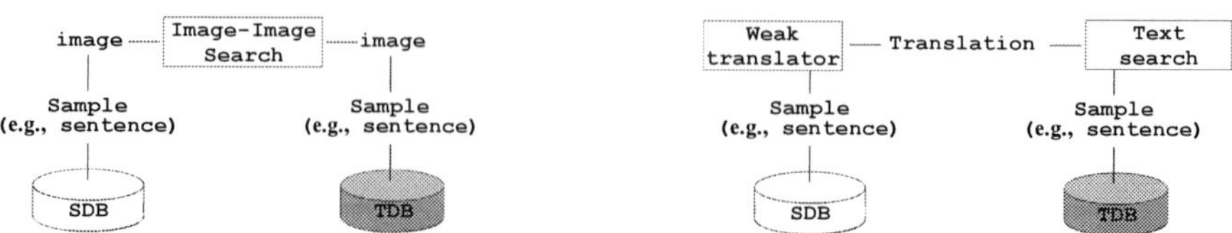

Figure 2: Frameworks of CMIR and CLIR. SDB is a source Data Bank (DB), while TDB a target DB.

To some extent, CMIR is easier to use than CLIR. The crucial issue for CMIR is only to improve the quality of the search results. CLIR needs to additionally consider the quality of the bilingual dictionaries or the performance of the weak translators.

In order to conduct CMIR, however, we need to ensure that there is indeed a correspondence between a pair of image and text. It means that the text sufficiently depicts the meanings of the image. To fulfil the requirement, we collect the images and their captions from the structure-fixed webpages, and use them to build the reliable data bank for CMIR.

In practice, we collect the pairs of images and captions from both the news websites in the source language and that in the target language, respectively building source Data Bank (SDB) and target Data Bank (TDB). Given a caption C_s in SDB and the corresponding image I_s, we calculated the image similarity between I_s and all images I_ts in TDB. Then we rank all I_ts based on image similarity. Finally we select the captions C_ts of the most highly ranked I_ts as the equivalents of C_s. The pairs of C_s and C_t are used as the bilingual sentence pairs to construct the comparable corpora.

3.2 Image-Image Search

The image-image search engine uses each of the images in the SDB as a query. For every query, the engine goes through all the images in the TDB and measures their visually similarity to the query. The similarity will be used as the criterion to rank the search results. In this paper, we employ the Scale-Invariant Feature Transformation method (SIFT) for representing the images, creating scale-invariant keypoint-centered feature vector. On the basis, we calculate the image similarity by using the Euclidean distance of the keypoints.

SIFT is an image characterization method, which has been proven to be more effective than other methods in detecting the local details from different perspectives at different scales. This advantage causes precise image-to-image matching. Figure 3 shows the theory behind SIFT.

The keypoints of the homogeneous images at different scales

The scale-invariant keypoints extracted by SIFT for the original image

Figure 3: SIFT process (assume that the biggest triangle is the original image). The keypoints are denoted by the directed square marks (the direction is denoted by the line that radiates outward from the middle of the square marks)

First, SIFT zooms in and out on the original image, so as to obtain the homogeneous images at different scales (see the three triangles at the left side of Figure 3). Second, SIFT extracts keypoints respectively in the homogeneous, and merges them to generate a set of scale-invariant keypoints (see those points in the triangle at the right side of Figure 3). The feature space which is instantiated by those scale-invariant keypoints is scale-independent, and therefore extremely conductive to detecting visually similar images at different scales (Lowe et al 1999, Lowe et al 2004).

SIFT employs the most distinctive point in a small area as a key feature, i.e., the so-called keypoint. Due to the local processing in different areas, SIFT is not only able to obtain locally optimal features but maintain all the similar key features occurred in different parts of the image.

Following the state-of-the-art SIFT (Lowe et al 2004, Yan et al 2004 and Hakim et al 2006) method, we define a small area as the set of a sampling point and the adjacent points (neighbours). It is noteworthy that the area includes not just the neighbours in the original image but those in the homogeneous images at different scales. We use Gaussian function to fit the size of all the points in the area. On the basis, we use the difference of Gaussian function to determine the extreme point, and specify the point as the distinctive point in the area.

Figure 4: Different versions of the top 5 image search results. They were respectively obtained when the threshold θ were finely turned from 0.6 to 0.9.

We model each keypoint by pixel-wise vectors in the keypoint-centered 16*16 windows. The vector represents both the direction and the value of image gradient. Lowe et al (2004) detail the gradient measurement method.

In total, we extract keypoints for the image representation. Given two images, we calculate the similarity by the average Euclidean distance of the matching keypoints. For a keypoint x in the source image, we determine the matching point in the target image by the following steps: First, we acquire two most similar keypoints y and z in the target image. Assume that the similarity of (x, y) is smaller than (x, z), second, we calculated the ratio r of the similarity $s(x, y)$ to $s(x, z)$. If r is bigger than a threshold θ, we determine that the keypoint z is the matching point of x; otherwise there isn't any matching point of x in the target image. We set the threshold θ as 0.8.

A smaller value of r $(r < \theta)$ will introduce many unqualified matching points in the image similarity calculation. It will reduce the precision of image search results. It means that most of the retrieved images are either dissimilar or unrelated. By contrast, a larger value causes few available matching points. It will influence the diversity of the search results. It means that most of the retrieved images are the same with each other or even extracted from the same provenances. Obviously, we would like to see that they derive from different `Medias` in different languages.

Figure 4 lists a series of images, which are the top 5 search results obtained by using different levels of θ. This group of search results are very representative in our experiments, able to reflect that the setting value 0.8 of θ is a reasonable boundary between correct and incorrect results. In particular, it can be found that such a threshold ensures the diversity of the correct results (Note that the query in this example is the left image in Figure 1).

3.3 Collecting and Processing Raw Data

We crawl the images and captions by using crawler4j[1], which is an open source toolkit specially developed for effectively crawling web data. On the basis, we use regular expressions to extract images and captions from the structured source files of the crawled web pages.

An optional preprocessing for an experimental system is to index images. It enables high-speed retrieval. We apply the locality-sensitive hashing (LSH) technique[2] for content-based image indexing.

4　Experiments

We conduct a pilot study for CMIR towards comparable corpora construction. The goal of this study is to verify whether image-image search is useful for the discovery of textual equivalents in TDB.

There is an important problem need to be solved firstly: *Reliability*. As mentioned in section 3.1, TDB is a data bank which contains a great number of images, along with the captions in the target language (named target captions for short). However, if we randomly select the captions in the source language (source captions) as the test samples for mining the bilingual captions, it is easy for us to encounter the problem that there is not a real equivalent in TDB. In the case, the experimental results are definitely unreliable. For example, the precision rate in the 5 highly-ranked target captions will always be 0. On the contrary however, if we added some ground-truth equivalents of the test samples to TDB, the experimental settings will be far from the real condition.

To solve the problem, we propose an automatic method of measuring comparability between source captions and target captions. Based on the measurement results, we collect pseudo ground-truth equivalents, and use them to enrich the test data. By this way, we can build an experimental environment similar to the real condition. We detail the method in section 4.4.

Besides, as usual, we show the corpus, traditional evaluation metrics and main experimental results one-by-one, which can be found in sections 4.1, 4.2 and 4.3. For the part of main result, we report the precision in top 5 highly-ranked target captions, as well as the ranking results, at four levels of comparability (parallel-level (abbr., `Par`.), comparable (`Com`.), pseudo-comparable (`Pse`.), and incomparable (`Inc`.)). In addition, we compare our method with the state-of-the-art CLIR method and the other image-image search engine.

4.1　Corpus

We crawled 42,633 images from Chinese news websites to initialize TDB. Each corresponds to a sole caption. The websites include China news, News of Sina and Xinhua Net (Chinese). In order to ensure sentence-level comparable corpora construction, we filtered the captions which are generated with multiple sentences or have a length of more than 20 Chinese words. Of course, the images of the captions were also filtered out of the TDB. Eventually, we obtained a TDB which contains 10,371 pairs of images and captions. As mentioned above, we didn't know whether there is an equivalent in the TDB for a source caption, and even if there does exist, we are blind to it (Black box).

We built a SDB (i.e., source data bank) in the same way. The source captions in the SDB are collected from the English news websites like online CNN, BBC and Xinhua Net (English). It is a mini-sized data bank, containing only 52 pairs of source captions and images (See their topics in Table1).

---

1 https://github.com/yasserg/crawler4j
2 https://github.com/embr/lsh

Honestly, this SDB can only support an English-Chinese CMIR (or CLIR), in which the English captions and the images serve as the queries. In our experiments, we use the queries as the test data.

Russia military parade/10	Russia Putin/10	Obama depart/10	Brazil Olympic/7	Greek migrant/10	Putin birth/10	Michelle/6	Pluto/8
Vehicle Afghanistan/10	Israel bomb/10	Obama Cuba/10	Artistic Korea/5	Curry Warrior/10	Taj Mahal/10	Ankara/10	Nepal/9
Ecuador earthquake/10	Leo Oscar/10	Earthquake/10	Obama meet/10	Prime Russia/4	Xing Zhan/8	Xi talk/10	Wolf/10
Mexico explosion/10	Hindu fire/10	Leonardo/10	NASA image/7	Angry birds/10	Kim speak/8	Baghdad/6	
Miss South Africa/9	Mitsubishi/10	Kon tiki2/5	North Korea/9	Prime Italy/4	Diamond/10	Volcano/8	
Brussels damage/10	Seattle fire/7	Rocket/10	Putin Kerry/10	Trump/5	Mh370/10	Whale/7	
Pakistan floods/10	Satellite/10	River/10	Queen birth/10	Kobe/10	Castro/10	Protest/7	

Table 1: The topics of the pairs of target images and captions in the SDB, along with the numbers of the equivalents in the TDB (They are listed in the format `topic/number`)

Towards the images in the SDB, we collect similar images in the Chinese news websites, and use them and their captions as the ground-truth data. By this way, we collect at least 5 equivalents (similar image and comparable caption) for each sample in the SDB. In total, we collect 451 ground-truth equivalents. We added them to the TDB. From here on, the TDB is no longer a black box for us. The correct and incorrect equivalents are the prior knowledge for evaluating the CMIR and CLIR systems.

4.2 Evaluation Metrics

We conduct our CMIR process in TDB, with the aim to verify whether CMIR is able to seek out the comparable target captions in a large-scale data set. This is the kernel of the proposed corpora construction method. If it is promising, we can accomplish the corpora construction by continuous CMIR using a massive number of source captions as the queries. Therefore we focus on evaluating the CMIR in this paper, using the samples in the mini-sized SDB as the queries.

The basic evaluation metric is the Precision rate (P). We didn't consider the Recall (R) rate. It is because that the genuine requirements of comparable corpora construction are the noise-free high-quality equivalents, but not all. Not just the acquisition of qualified equivalents, P@N also reflects the ability of a CMIR (or CLIR) system to filter incorrect equivalents out of the top n search results.

4.3 Main Results

We rank the retrieved target captions (candidate equivalents) by CMIR in terms of image similarity, and evaluate the performance in the top-n ($1 \leq n \leq 5$) highly ranked target captions. Table 2 shows the performance (P@n). Besides, we compare our method with Talvensaari et al (2007)'s CLIR system. Note that the listed performance in the table is the Macro precision among the 52 test samples.

As shown in Table 2, CMIR achieves promising results. The precision in the top 5 search results is more than 60%. Besides, CMIR outperforms the state of the art CLIR, yielding nearly 2% performance gains at top 1 and in top 2.

	#P@1	#P@2	#P@3	#P@4	#P@5
CMIR (SIFT)	**0.846**	**0.788**	0.718	0.658	0.615
CLIR	0.827	0.769	0.756	0.745	0.703

Table 2: Main test results (Precision rates in top-n equivalents) for both CMIR and CLIR

It is easy to raise a question of whether the degree of comparability of source and target captions is proportionate to the similarity of their images. If it does, we can conclude that CMIR is conductive to the acquisition of high-quality equivalents. In order to answer the question, we verify the distributions of different levels of equivalents over the image-similarity based rankings. We consider four levels of equivalents, including Par, Com, Pse, and Inc. Note that the levels were manually annotated beforehand. Table 3 shows their definitions and a concrete example for each. A smaller sequence number in the ranking list implies a higher image similarity. For example, the image of the ranked 1st target caption (top equivalent) is most similar to the corresponding image of the source caption. Figure 5 shows the distributions for the rankings from 1 to 5.

Definition of `Par.`: Two sentences are the translation of each other or approximate translation with minor variations, which can be aligned on the word level. (see examples as below)
(English) *Italian Prime Minister Matteo Renzi meets with visiting Chinese Foreign Minister Wang Yi in Rome, Italy, on May 5, 2016. /*
(Chinese) 5 月 5 日/*May 5,* 意大利/*Italy* 总理/*premier* 伦齐/*Renzi* 在/*at* 罗马/*Rome* 会见/*meet with* 中国/*Chinese* 外交部长/*foreign minister* 王毅/*Yi Wang.*
Definition of `Com.`: Two sentences in different languages depict the same event or topic, from very similar perspectives. One contains the translations of most constituents of the other. (see examples as below)
(English) *Flash floods in Pakistan and Kashmir Kill at Least 53.*
(Chinese) 巴基斯坦/*Pakistan* 爆发/*break* 洪灾/*flood* 和/*and* 山体/*mountain* 滑坡/*landslides* 至少/*at least 53/53* 死/*dead 60/60* 伤/*injury.*
Definition of `Pse.`: The sentences present the same event or topic from very different perspectives. They only contain several semantically equivalent words or phrases. (see examples as below)
(English) *people take photos of bodies of dead stranded sperm whales behind the dyke of Kaiser Wilhelm Koog.*
(Chinese) 8/8 头/*number* 抹香鲸/*sperm whale* 搁浅/*stranded* 德国/*Germany* 海滩/*sea beach* 起重机/*crane* 运输/*transport* 尸体/*corpse.*

Table 3: Definitions of the parallel-level (`Par.`), comparable (`Com.`) and pseudo-comparable (`Pse.`) equivalents, along with the examples. The rest cases are specified as incomparable (`Inc.`) sentences.

It can be found that most of the lower-level equivalents (`Pse` and `Inc`) were ranked at the bottom of the ranking list: more than 69% of `Pse`-level equivalents won the 3rd, 4th and 5th places, and 88% `Inc` won the same places (see the left diagram in Figure 5). On the contrary, most of the higher-level equivalents (`Par` and `Com`) were ranked at the top: more than 66% of `Par`-level equivalents won the 1st, 2nd and 3rd places, and 78% of `Com` won the same places. It illustrates that CMIR is able to distinguish the high-quality equivalents from the low-quality, and rank the former to the top of the ranking list. It helps a translator finely tune the proportions of comparable samples of different qualifies in a bilingual corpora as requirement, e.g., noise-free smaller-sized corpora or large-scale noisy corpora (The former are reliable but provide less translation knowledge, the latter are just the opposite).

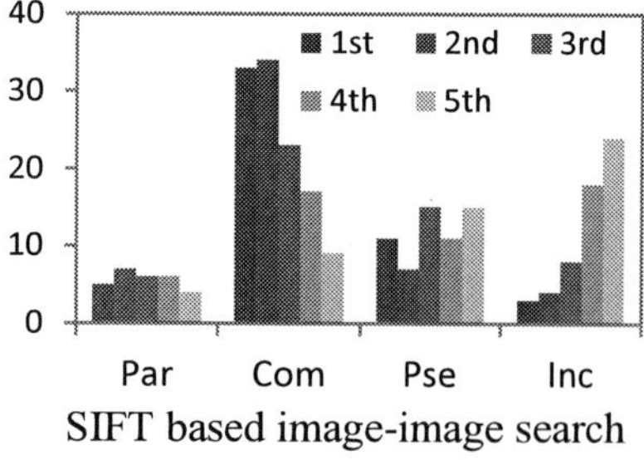

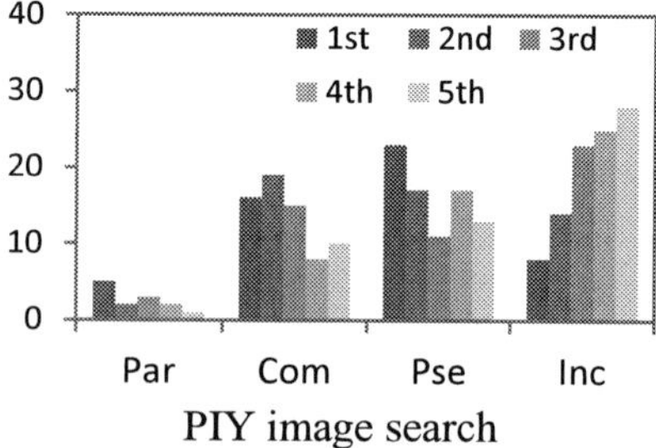

Figure 5: Distributions of different levels (`Par`, `Com`, `Pse` and `Inc`) of equivalents over the image-similarity based rankings. Exhibited in the left diagram are the distributions of the retrieved equivalents by our SIFT based image-image search engine, while the right by PIY image search. Each column in the histogram denotes the number of certain level of equivalents that arrive at the same ranking.

Considering the important influence of image-image search to translation-oriented CMIR, we conduct an additional experiment to evaluate different image search engines. We employ an open-source engine, named PIY[3], which is a well-developed and easy to use. PIY calculates image similarity by using 3D colour histogram. Figure 5 shows the performance of the PIY based CMIR (see the right diagram). It can be found that PIY has the same advantage with our CMIR method, capable of raising high-quality equivalents in the search results. Nevertheless, PIY achieved a worse precision in top-5 search results. The macro-average precision is 0.5, far below the performance of our method.

---

3 http://www.pyimagesearch.com/2014/12/08/adding-web-interface-image-search-engine-flask/

4.4 Collaborative Evaluation

We propose an automatic method to measure the comparability between a source caption and the target (a candidate equivalent). The method can be used to evaluate the results of CMIR without knowing the ground truth. It measures the comparability by using the following features:

- Content similarity (f_c) is calculated by the Cosine measure between TFIDF based VSM models of source caption and target caption (Only content words are considered in the calculation).
- Co-occurrence of entities (f_e) is calculated by the joint co-occurrence rates of entity mentions in source caption and target caption.
- Length ratio (f_l) is the difference of the length of the captions. If they have the same length, f_l is equal to 1, otherwise a smaller value (divide the length of the shorter by that of the longer)

On the basis, we measure the comparability by combing the features by the linear weighted sum method: $C=\alpha \cdot f_c + \beta \cdot f_e + \gamma \cdot f_l$, where the parameters α, β and γ are empirically set as 0.8, 0.15 and 0.05. Further, we divide the ground-truth samples (i.e., bilingual caption pairs) into three classes in terms of the prior level of comparability, i.e., `Par`, `Com` and `Pse`. For each class, we calculate the average C. Table 3 shows the calculation results. It can be found that the average C-measure of the classes of the ground truth closely fit the manual ratings of the classes (the rating score 3 corresponds to the `Par`-level, 2 to `Com` and 1 to `Pse`). The Pearson factor between the ratings and the C scores is high up to 0.99. It illustrates that the trend of gradient descent of C is similar to that of manual ratings.

	#Par.	#Com.	#Pse.	Pearson
Rating	3.0	2.0	1.0	0.993
C-measure	0.646	0.496	0.397	

Table 3: Comparability C-measure and Pearson parameter

Accordingly, we use C-measure to ensure the reliability of the evaluation process when there is lack of known ground-truth equivalents. We set $\vartheta(C, \varepsilon)$ as a linear function of the deviation ε from the average C-measure of certain level of equivalents: $\vartheta(C, \varepsilon)=C-a \cdot \varepsilon$. We estimate the optimal factor a in the training data by maximizing the precision. We use $\vartheta(C, \varepsilon)$ as the criteria to determine whether a target caption is a qualified equivalent for a certain level of comparability. For example, if $C(x, y) > \vartheta(C, \varepsilon)$, x is comparable to y (at `Par`-level, `Com` or `Pse`). The qualified equivalents will be used as the ground-truth data to evaluate the performance of the CMIR systems.

An instantiated $\vartheta(C, \varepsilon)$ enables an experiment on large-scale test data (source captions as queries) and rich ground-truth data. The test result, therefore, will be more reliable than the current case. Active learning can be applied for enhancing the evaluation process.

5 Conclusion

In this paper, we propose a CMIR method to obtain bilingual sentence pairs, with the aim to construct sentence-level comparable corpora. The CMIR applies SIFT algorithm for image similarity measurement. On the basis, it detects the captions of similar images in source data and target data, as use them as search results. Experiments show that CMIR is promising in acquiring the comparable captions.

In the future, we will focus on the implement of a CMIR-based corpora constructor. The first difficulty for us is to determine the source captions that indeed have at least one equivalent in TDB. Obviously, the CMIR results for other source captions all are incorrect. If add them to the corpora, the quality of the data set will be reduced largely. The resolution is to use burst measurement method to detect break news, and use the captions and images in the news stories as the source data. It may work well because that break news would be reported widely around the world. There should be always some topic-related stories occurred in the news websites in the target language. This largely increases the probability that target data contain the desired equivalents.

Another crucial issue is to predict the numbers of the target captions which will be added to the corpora. A possible solution is to measure the textual comparability for a massive number of highly ranked target captions, and use $\vartheta(C, \varepsilon)$ as the threshold to filter out the `Inc`-level samples. However this method will negatively influence efficiency. Nevertheless, this problem may raise an interest in the joint model of textual comparability and image similarity, as well as collaboration methods.

Acknowledgements

This research is supported by the U.S. DARPA DEFT Program (No. FA8750-13-2-0041), ARL NS-CTA (No. W911NF-09-2-0053), NSF CA-REER Award (IIS-1523198), and the National Natural Science Foundation of China, No.61672368, No.61373097, No.61672367, No.61272259. The authors would like to thank the anonymous reviewers for their insightful comments and suggestions. The views and conclusions contained in this document are those of the authors and should not be interpreted as representing the official policies, either expressed or implied, of the U.S. and CHN Governments. The U.S. and CHN Governments are authorized to reproduce and distribute reprints for Government purposes notwithstanding any copyright notation here on. Yu Hong, Professor Associate in Soochow University, is the corresponding author of the paper, whose email address is tianxianer@gmail.com.

Reference

Abdel Hakim, Alaa Elvalser, and Aly A. Farag. 2006. CSIFT: A SIFT descriptor with color invariant characteristics. Conference on Computer Vision and Pattern Recognition, pages 1345-1354.

Abdul Rauf, Sadaf, and Holger Schwenk. 2009. On the use of comparable corpora to improve SMT performance. In Proceedings of the 12th Conference of the European Chapter of the Association for Computational Linguistics, pages 16–23.

Bo Li and Eric Gaussier. 2010. Improving corpus comparability for bilingual lexicon extraction from comparable corpora. In Proceedings of the 23rd International Conference on Computational Linguistics, pages 644–652.

Degen Huang, Lian Zhao, Lishuang Li, and Haitao Yu. 2010. Mining large-scale comparable corpora from chinese-english news collections. In Proceedings of the 23rd International Conference on Computational Linguistics, pages 472–480.

Fangzhong Su and Bogdan Babych. 2012. Development and application of a cross-language document comparability metric. In Proceedings of the 8th International Conference on Language Resources and Evaluation, pages 3956–3962.

Hashemi, Homa B, and Azadeh Shakery. 2014. Mining a Persian–English comparable corpus for cross-language information retrieval. Information Processing & Management, pages 384-398.

Irvine Ann, Chris Callison Burch. 2014. Using comparable corpora to adapt mt models to new domains. In Proceedings of the 9th Workshop on Statistical Machine Translation, pages 437–444.

Inguna Skadiņa, Ahmet Aker, Nikos Mastropavlos, Fangzhong Su. 2012. Collecting and using comparable corpora for statistical machine translation. In Proceedings of the 8th International Conference on Language Resources and Evaluation, pages 438-445.

Judita Preiss. 2012. Identifying comparable corpora using lda. In Proceedings of the 2012 Conference of the North American Chapter of the Association for Computational Linguistics: Human Language Technologies, pages 558–562.

Ke, Yan, and Rahul Sukthankar. 2004. PCA-SIFT: A more distinctive representation for local image descriptors. Conference on Computer Vision and Pattern Recognition, pages 456-466.

Lowe David. 1999. Object recognition from local scale-invariant features. The proceedings of the 7th IEEE International Conference on Computer vision, pages 1150-1157.

Morin, Emmanuel, and Emmanuel Prochasson. 2011. Bilingual lexicon extraction from comparable corpora enhanced with parallel corpora. In Proceedings of the 4th Workshop on Building and Using Comparable Corpora, 49th Annual Meeting of the Association for Computational Linguistics, pages 27–34.

Pablo Gamallo Otero and Isaac González López. 2010. Wikipedia as multilingual source of comparable corpora. In Proceedings of the 3rd Workshop on Building and Using Comparable Corpora, pages 21–25.

Pal Santanu, Partha Pakray, and Sudip Kumar Naskar. 2014. Automatic building and using parallel resources for SMT from comparable corpora. In Proceedings of 3rd Workshop on Hybrid Approaches to Translation (HyTra) @ EACL 2014, pages 48–57.

Jason R. Smith, Chris Quirk, and Kristina Toutanova. 2010. Extracting parallel sentences from comparable corpora using document level alignment. Human Language Technologies: The 2010 Annual Conference of the North American Chapter of the Association for Computational Linguistics.

Tuomas Talvensaari, Jorma Laurikkala, Kalervo Järvelin, Martti Juhola, and Heikki Keskustalo. 2007. Creating and exploiting a comparable corpus in cross-language information retrieval. ACM Transactions on Information Systems, 25(1):4.

Xiaochuan Ni, Jian-Tao Sun, Jian Hu, and Zheng Chen. 2009. Mining multilingual topics from wikipedia. In Proceedings of the 18th International Conference on World Wide Web, pages 1155–1156.

Zede Zhu, Miao Li, Lei Chen, and Zhenxin Yang. 2013. Building comparable corpora based on bilingual lda model. In Proceedings of the 51st Annual Meeting of the Association for Computational Linguistics, pages 278–282.

Predicting Translation Equivalents in Linked WordNets

Krasimir Angelov
University of Gothenburg
`krasimir@chalmers.se`

Gleb Lobanov
Chalmers / Gothenburg
`mail@gleblobanov.ru`

Abstract

We present an algorithm for predicting translation equivalents between two languages, based on the corresponding WordNets. The assumption is that all synsets of one of the languages are linked to the corresponding synsets in the other language. In theory, given the exact sense of a word in a context it must be possible to translate it as any of the words in the linked synset. In practice, however, this does not work well since automatic and accurate sense disambiguation is difficult. Instead it is possible to define a more robust translation relation between the lexemes of the two languages. As far as we know the Finnish WordNet is the only one that includes that relation. Our algorithm can be used to predict the relation for other languages as well. This is useful for instance in hybrid machine translation systems which are usually more dependent on high-quality translation dictionaries.

1 Introduction

High-quality translation dictionaries are an indispensable resource in both language technology and language learning applications. For instance, rule-based translation systems (Forcada et al., 2011; Angelov et al., 2014; Mayor et al., 2011; Popel and Žabokrtský, 2010) rely on high-quality dictionaries. Unlike statistical translation systems, the rule-based systems are a lot more vulnerable to noise in the translation model, since the disambiguation is done by rules that are partly or fully manually designed. On the contrary, noise in statistical systems could be suppressed if the model can learn that the suspicious entries are very unlikely. Even when rule-based systems are supplemented with statistical ranking as in Angelov et al. (2014), it is still desirable to reduce the noise in the dictionary. For example the system in Angelov et al. (2014) offers direct access to the dictionary to the user, which is useful for language learning purposes, but only when the dictionary has a very high-quality.

Getting a high-quality resource is not easy. In this paper we look into transforming existing WordNets into translation dictionaries. WordNet offers rich intra-lingual semantic information and when several WordNets are linked to the original Princeton WordNet (Fellbaum, 1998) then, all together, they form an unique interlingual resource. Extraction of the rough translations from one language to another is possible by going via the English senses as a pivot.

The problem is that the translations that we get from WordNet are very liberal. Lets take an example. When looking for the word *house* in Princeton WordNet, we see this as one of the possible synsets:

1. (n) family, household, house, home, menage
       (a social unit living together)

which is linked to the following synset in Spanish:

2. (n) casa, hogar, familia
       (a social unit living together)

Now it should be obvious that it is quite nave to believe that each word in the English synset is equally good translation to each Spanish word from the linked synset. For example translating *family* to *familia* is very likely to be correct independently from the context, while the replacement of *family* with *casa* would be appropriate only if the intended meaning of *family* is the sense that is represented with this synset. Sometimes even this is not enough. For instance, one of the examples for the synset is:

Proceedings of the Sixth Workshop on Hybrid Approaches to Translation,
pages 26–32, Osaka, Japan, December 11, 2016.

```
He moved his family to Virginia.
```

If we translate *family* to *casa*, this will trigger the other sense of *casa* as a kind of building, which is not shared with the word *family*. In general, the translation relation is a subset of the relation that we get from the linked synsets.

Unfortunately, to our knowledge, the Finnish WordNet (Lindén and Carlson, 2010) is the only one which encodes the translatability on the word level. We used the translation relation from the Finnish WordNet as a gold standard, and we looked at different features which can help us to predict which pairs of words from any two linked synsets are likely to be good translation pairs. It turned out that these features are mostly language-independent which means that we can use them to classify word pairs from other languages. We did a pilot experiment for English-Russian which gave us promising results.

2   Predicting the Translation Relation

The discussion from the previous section hints at the first possible classification feature. Different words are characterized by different sets of senses. Two words from different languages that share most of their possible senses are more likely to be considered as translational equivalents than two other which share fewer senses. The intuition is obvious. In the ideal case when the two words have exactly the same senses, then translating one with the other will never be wrong. This are ideal translation equivalents. In a more realistic situation the words share only some senses, but more shared senses means lower chance of making mistake. Using nearly ideal translation equivalents makes the automatic translation more robust since errors in the sense disambiguation are less likely to lead to wrong translations.

If we take for example the synsets 1 and 2 from the previous section, then Table 1 shows for every pair of English/Spanish words their co-occurrence counts. The list is sorted in the order of decreasing counts. We see that there are five linked synsets which contain the English word *family* and the Spanish equivalent *familia*. The same is true for *house–casa* and *home–casa*. There are only four synsets which contain the combination *house–hogar*. All other combinations appear in only one synset, i.e. only in the one that we have taken as an example. The last column in the table shows the sorting rank for each pair.

We use the following two-step selection algorithm:

1. Go downwards through the sorted list and add as translation candidates all pairs of words where for neither of the two words there is already a chosen translation.

2. If there is a word in either language for which in the previous step we have not selected any translation, then attach it to the word in the other language for which the corresponding pair appears up-most in the list.

The first step selects the word pairs with the highest possible co-occurrence counts. The second step ensures that no word is left without translation. Following the algorithm we see that these pairs will be selected as the best translations:

family – familia	*household – casa*
house – casa	*menage – casa*
home – hogar	

The first two pairs *family – familia* and *house – casa* are simply on the top of the ranked list on Table 1. The third pair in the list *home – casa*, must be ignored because we have already used *casa* in the previous translations. The next pair then is *home – hogar*. None of the other pairs can be selected in the first step because we have already used all Spanish words.

There are still the words *household* and *menage* for which there is no translation. The second step considers those. The upmost appearance of both *household* and *menage* links those with *casa*. Note that the role of the second step is merely to ensure that all words get some translation. This mimics the design in the Finnish WordNet which strives to give a translation for all words. As it could be seen in this particular example, however, the selections done by the second step are less than ideal. Neither *household* nor *menage* are good translations of *casa* outside of this very particular sense.

Note that there is an ambiguity here. For example both *house – casa* and *home – casa* are of rank 1 which means that whether *house* or *home* will be selected as translation of *casa* is arbitrary. We could

English	Spanish	Count	Rank
family	familia	5	1
house	casa	5	1
home	casa	5	1
home	hogar	4	2
family	casa	1	3
family	hogar	1	3
household	casa	1	3
household	familia	1	3
household	hogar	1	3
house	familia	1	3
house	hogar	1	3
home	familia	1	3
menage	casa	1	3
menage	familia	1	3
menage	hogar	1	3

Table 1: Co-occurrence counts

English	Spanish	Distance	Rank
animal	animal	0	1
fauna	fauna	0	1
creature	criatura	2	2
beast	bestia	3	3
brute	bestia	4	4
brute	fauna	4	4
animal	fauna	5	5
beast	fauna	5	5
fauna	animal	5	5
fauna	bestia	5	5
fauna	criatura	5	5
animal	bestia	6	6
beast	animal	6	6
brute	animal	6	6
brute	criatura	6	6
creature	bestia	6	6
creature	fauna	6	6
animal	criatura	7	7
beast	criatura	7	7
animate being	animal	8	8
creature	animal	8	8
animate being	criatura	10	9
animate being	bestia	11	10
animate being	fauna	11	10

Table 2: Levenshtein distance

collect them both as alternative translations, but in the final algorithm we also use other features which means that the possibility for ambiguity is reduced.

A very common ambiguity arises when too many pairs from the same synset have co-occurrence count one. This means that these pairs appear only in the current synset and the count is useless. In that case one feature that we can use without involving external resources is the word similarity. It turns out that many of the words that have only one synset are often technical terms and they are often borrowed from one language to another. This means that the translations are usually lexically very similar. To capture that, we can rank the word pairs by their Levenshtein (1966) distance. It is very important, however, that the distance is used only inside a single synset. If we instead use it globally then it would also capture a lot of false friends, i.e. words that sound similar but have completely different meanings. False friends, however, should never be in the same synset if the WordNet data is accurate.

Let's consider the following linked synsets in English:

3. (n) animal, animate being, beast, brute, creature, fauna
        (a living organism characterized by voluntary movement)

and in Spanish:

4. (n) animal, criatura, bestia, fauna
        (a living organism characterized by voluntary movement)

The list of all possible translation pairs is shown in Table 2, together with the Levenshtein distance between the two words. Note that while the co-occurrence list was sorted in descending order, here we use the order of increasing distance since we prefer words that are lexically more similar. The last column on the table shows the rank which now increases with the distance.

Looking at the table it is easy to see that the best candidates for translations are:

0.92	**0.58**	0.41	0.34	0.30	0.24	0.21	0.17	0.15	0.14	0.12	0.11	0.10	0.11	0.09	0.09
0.64	0.37	0.31	0.25	0.22	0.20	0.18	0.18	0.15	0.14	0.12	0.10	0.09	0.07	0.07	0.07
0.38	0.27	0.24	0.21	0.18	0.17	0.15	0.16	0.14	0.15	0.14	0.09	0.11	0.10	0.00	0.07
0.25	0.20	0.20	0.18	0.17	0.15	0.14	0.14	0.12	0.11	0.12	0.09	0.04	0.00	0.00	0.00
0.22	0.18	0.18	0.15	0.16	0.12	0.14	0.14	0.12	0.15	0.12	0.15	0.04	0.00	0.00	0.33
0.19	0.16	0.16	0.14	0.20	0.08	0.11	0.27	0.18	0.15	0.18	0.00	0.00	0.00	0.00	0.00
0.25	0.00	0.22	0.00	0.14	0.00	**0.50**	0.00	0.00	**1.00**	0.00	0.00	0.00	0.00	0.00	0.00

Table 3: The translation probability as a function of the Levenshtein rank (columns) and the co-occurrence rank (rows)

animal – animal	animate being – criatura
fauna – fauna	brute – bestia
creature – criatura	
beast – bestia	

The words *animal* and *fauna* are simply identical in English and Spanish, while the pairs *creature – criatura* and *beast – bestia* are almost the same. The words in the first column are selected in the first step of the algorithm and the second column is added by the second step. Obviously the first step has captured all clear translations, while for the second step the Levenshtein distance is not of a much help, and it gives more or less arbitrary assignments.

The Levenshtein distance makes sense only for languages using the same script. If the scripts are different then one of the languages must be transliterated. For example, for Russian we used a transliteration that is compliant with ISO 9 (ISO, 1995). For other languages like Chinese and Japanese using transliteration would probably make very little sense. In general the Levenshtein distance is more useful for closely related languages than for more distinct ones.

The third feature that we have considered is the joint alignment probability estimated from a parallel corpus with GIZA. Unfortunately, an evaluation on Finnish has shown that using the alignment probability only makes things worse. The reason is that there were far too many zero counts (sparse data) and when we actually have a non-zero count it is often noise. This happens for instance when the corpus contains paraphrases rather than direct translations. At the end when using only the alignment probability, the overall accuracy of the prediction was low, and when it is used together with other features it made the prediction slightly worse.

Now we have two useful ranks for every word pair. The first is based on the co-occurrence count and the second on the Levenshtein distance. Both rankings are advantageous in different cases and somehow we should use them together. Instead of using the ranks for selection directly, we used them as features in a probabilistic classifier. The Finnish WordNet (Lindén and Carlson, 2010) lists directly the translations on word-to-word basis. We used that data to estimate the probability that a word pair with given co-occurrence and distance ranks is a translation. The probabilities are shown on Table 3. The columns correspond to different distance ranks and the rows to different co-occurrence ranks.

In the table we have highlighted combinations with probability greater than 0.50. It is obvious that most true translations are gathered close to the upper left corner, i.e. where both ranks are with value either 1 or 2. The two outliers on the last row are just coincidences where there is only one pair with those ranks and it happened to be a true translation. The table confirms our assumption that the two features that we designed are useful in selecting translation pairs.

Once we have the table we can use the probability as a combined rank instead of the individual co-occurrence and distance ranks. For each pair we compute the two ranks and then we lookup the translation probability from the table. The list of word pairs is then sorted by decreasing probability.

It is interesting that although the table is estimated on Finnish it can be used with any other pair of languages. Once the two ranks are computed on the language dependent data, there is nothing language specific in the two numbers. The probability table however is not completely language independent. We could for instance guess that for languages with very different lexical structure, the translation probability will decrease slowly with the Levenshtein distance than for a closely related pair. Nevertheless, we used the table for predicting translations for Finnish, Russian, Slovenian and Spanish. For now, however, we

		Manual	
		Translation	Not Translation
Algorithm	Translation	43.10%	8.38%
	Not Translation	9.76%	38.76%

Precision: 83.72% Recall: 81.54% Accuracy: 81.86%

Table 4: Evaluation of algorithm's ability to determine translation pairs for Finnish

		Manual	
		Translation	Not Translation
Algorithm	Translation	37.57%	26.43%
	Not Translation	15.29%	20.72%

Precision: 58.70% Recall: 71.07% Accuracy: 58.29%

Table 5: Evaluation of algorithm's ability to determine translation pairs for Finnish with word alignment

have done quantitative evaluation only on Finnish and Russian.

2.1 Evaluation

To generate a translation dictionary, we need two linked WordNets. The Open Multilingual WordNet (Bond and Paik, 2012) bundles together the WordNets for dosens of languages. In addition Bond and Foster (2013) have extended the database with data for plenty of other languages that is automatically learned from Wiktionary.

In particular we have used the WordNets for English (Fellbaum, 1998), Russian, Slovenian (Fišer et al., 2012), Spanish (Gonzalez-Agirre et al., 2012) and Finnish (Lindén and Carlson, 2010). The WordNet for Russian comes from the automatic extension and is thus much smaller and less reliable. When looking for other Russian WordNets connected with Princeton WordNet, we also found the RussNet (Azarova et al., 2002), Yet Another RussNet (Braslavski et al., 2016), and Russian WordNet (Lipatov et al., 2016). Unfortunately, none of these is linked to any other WordNet. Furthermore, only the Yet Another RussNet and the Russian WordNet are freely available.

We did quantitative evaluation on Finnish and Russian. For the other languages we only checked a few occasional examples which were reasonable but we did not do more thorough evaluation.

For Finnish, we used the gold standard translation relation that the Finnish WordNet provides, and we applied 10-fold cross-validation. We used a table similar to the one on Table 3 but computed on a randomly selected 9/10 of the data. The remaining 1/10 was used for evaluation. The evaluation results, averaged over 10 random selections, are shown on Table 4. The overall accuracy of the model is 81.86%. For comparison, choosing random translation pairs gives only about 50% accuracy.

For Finnish, we also tried to use GIZA alignment probabilities estimated from EuroParl (Koehn, 2005). Before the alignment the corpus was lemmatized and part-of-speech tagged with the TreeTagger (Schmid, 1994). Unfortunately, as we can see on Table 5 the accuracy of the probabilities as a feature is very low – 58.29%. Most of that can be attributed to sparse data and noise. Because of the low accuracy we excluded the alignment from the further experiments.

For Russian, there was no existing gold standard data. For the automatic prediction we used the numbers on Table 3 that are computed on the whole data set for Finnish. For the evaluation, we used the expertise of a native speaker. We decided to select all translation pairs that contain the most frequent 101 English words based on the English section of the OpenSubtitles corpus (Lison and Tiedemann, 2016). The total number of pairs amounts to 1010 and the evaluator was asked to decide whether this is a good translation or not. After that the results from the algorithm were compared with the manual evaluation.

The evaluation for Russian (Table 6) shows an accuracy of 60.78%. This is much lower than the

		Manual	
		Translation	Not Translation
Algorithm	Translation	28.21%	20.39%
	Not Translation	18.81%	32.5%

Precision: 58.05% Recall: 60.00% Accuracy: 60.71%

Table 6: Evaluation of algorithm's ability to determine translation pairs for Russian

results for Finnish. However, it is unfair to compare the two numbers for at least three reasons. The first is that the Russian WordNet (20 138 synsets) is much smaller than the one for Finnish (116 763). This strongly affects the predictive power of the co-occurrence counts, since more of them are just equal to one. The other reason is that while the Finnish WordNet is manually created and it is properly validated, the Russian WordNet is created automatically from Wiktionary. It is possible that it contains noise that affects the results. Lastly, we choose to evaluate only the most frequent words. This is useful since potential errors found in the evaluation can be fixed by hand and fixing the most frequent words will improve the quality of the final translation dictionary the most. However, these words are also more difficult to translate and thus the algorithm might be more susceptible to making errors. The evaluation shows the behaviour of the algorithm in a very unfavorable situation and it still shows positive results.

3   Implementation and Applications

The algorithm was implemented in Haskell and is available on GitHub:

```
http://www.grammaticalframework.org/lib/src/translator/classify.hs
```

After execution, it generates a table consisting of all possible pairs for the two languages together with a prediction of whether this is a real translation equivalent or not. By using other programs, the translation equivalents are further processed to generate translation dictionaries usable in the GF Offline Translator (Angelov et al., 2014).

4   Conclusion

Our work is not the first example where WordNet is used as translation dictionary. However, previous uses were dependent on sense disambiguation in the translation pipe line (see Virk et al. (2014) for example). While we still need sense disambiguation, it can be made more robust by choosing better translation pairs. If sense distinctions that does not lead to different translations are merged, then the disambiguator can work on the level of more coarse word senses. In contrast the WordNet senses are often said to be too fine-grained for automatic disambiguation.

Acknowledgements

This work is partly supported by the Swedish Research Council (Vetenskapsradet) under grant agreement number 2012-4506 and the Lars Pareto Travel Grant.

References

Krasimir Angelov, Aarne Ranta, and Björn Bringert. 2014. Speech-enabled hybrid multilingual translation for mobile devices. In *European Chapter of the Association for Computational Linguistics*, Gothenburg.

Irina Azarova, Olga Mitrofanova, Anna Sinopalnikova, Maria Yavorskaya, and Ilya Oparin. 2002. RussNet: Building a lexical database for the russian language. In *In: Proceedings: Workshop on Wordnet Structures and Standardisation and How this affect Wordnet Applications and Evaluation. Las Palmas*, pages 60–64.

Francis Bond and Ryan Foster. 2013. Linking and extending an open multilingual wordnet. In *In 51st Annual Meeting of the Association for Computational Linguistics: ACL-2013*, pages 1352–1362, Sofia.

Francis Bond and Kyonghee Paik. 2012. A survey of wordnets and their licenses. In *Proceedings of the 6th Global WordNet Conference (GWC 2012)*, pages 64–71.

P. Braslavski, D. Ustalov, M. Mukhin, and Y. Kiselev. 2016. Yarn: Spinning-in-progress. In *Proceedings of the Eight Global Wordnet Conference*, pages 58–65, Bucharest, Romania.

Christiane Fellbaum. 1998. *WordNet: An Electronic Lexical Database*. MIT Press.

Darja Fišer, Jernej Novak, and Tomaž. 2012. sloWNet 3.0: development, extension and cleaning. In *Proceedings of 6th International Global Wordnet Conference (GWC 2012)*, pages 113–117. The Global WordNet Association.

Mikel L. Forcada, Mireia Ginesti-Rosell, Jacob Nordfalk, Jim O'Regan, Sergio Ortiz-Rojas, JuanAntonio Perez-Ortiz, Felipe Sanchez-Martinez, Gema Ramirez-Sanchez, and FrancisM. Tyers. 2011. Apertium: a free/open-source platform for rule-based machine translation. *Machine Translation*, 25(2):127–144.

Aitor Gonzalez-Agirre, Egoitz Laparra, and German Rigau. 2012. Multilingual central repository version 3.0: upgrading a very large lexical knowledge base. In *Proceedings of the 6th Global WordNet Conference (GWC 2012)*, Matsue.

ISO. 1995. Information and documentation – transliteration of cyrillic characters into latin characters – slavic and non-slavic languages. Standard, International Organization for Standardization, March.

Philipp Koehn. 2005. Europarl: A Parallel Corpus for Statistical Machine Translation. In *Conference Proceedings: the tenth Machine Translation Summit*, pages 79–86, Phuket, Thailand. AAMT, AAMT.

V. I. Levenshtein. 1966. Binary Codes Capable of Correcting Deletions, Insertions and Reversals. *Soviet Physics Doklady*, 10:707, February.

Krister Lindén and Lauri Carlson. 2010. FinnWordNet - WordNet på finska via översättning. *LexicoNordica - Nordic Journal of Lexicography*, 17:119–140.

Anton Lipatov, Artem Goncharuk, Ilja Gelfenbejn, Viktor Shilo, and Vlad Lehelt. 2016. Russian wordnet, http://wordnet.ru.

Pierre Lison and Jörg Tiedemann. 2016. Opensubtitles2016: Extracting large parallel corpora from movie and TV subtitles. In Nicoletta Calzolari, Khalid Choukri, Thierry Declerck, Sara Goggi, Marko Grobelnik, Bente Maegaard, Joseph Mariani, Hélène Mazo, Asunción Moreno, Jan Odijk, and Stelios Piperidis, editors, *Proceedings of the Tenth International Conference on Language Resources and Evaluation LREC 2016, Portorož, Slovenia, May 23-28, 2016*. European Language Resources Association (ELRA).

Aingeru Mayor, Iñaki Alegria, Arantza Díaz de Ilarraza, Gorka Labaka, Mikel Lersundi, and Kepa Sarasola. 2011. Matxin, an open-source rule-based machine translation system for basque. *Machine Translation*, 25(1):53–82.

Martin Popel and Zdeněk Žabokrtský, 2010. *TectoMT: Modular NLP Framework*, pages 293–304. Springer Berlin Heidelberg, Berlin, Heidelberg.

Helmut Schmid. 1994. Probabilistic part-of-speech tagging using decision trees.

Shafqat Mumtaz Virk, KVS Prasad, Aarne Ranta, and Krasimir Angelov. 2014. Developing an interlingual translation lexicon using wordnets and grammatical framework. *COLING 2014*, page 55.

Modifications of Machine Translation Evaluation Metrics by Using Word Embeddings

Haozhou Wang
Department of Linguistics
University of Geneva
`Haozhou.Wang@etu.unige.ch`

Paola Merlo
Department of Linguistics
University of Geneva
`Paola.Merlo@unige.ch`

Abstract

Traditional machine translation evaluation metrics such as BLEU and WER have been widely used, but these metrics have poor correlations with human judgements because they badly represent word similarity and impose strict identity matching. In this paper, we propose some modifications to the traditional measures based on word embeddings for these two metrics. The evaluation results show that our modifications significantly improve their correlation with human judgements.

1 Introduction

One of the challenges for Machine Translation (MT) research is how to evaluate the quality of translations automatically and correctly. Earlier word-based metrics such as BLEU (Papineni et al., 2002), WER and TER (Snover et al., 2006) have been widely used in machine translation, but these metrics have poor correlations with human judgements, especially at the sentence level. One reason is that they just allow strict string matchings between hypothesis and references. For example, the semantically related words "learn" and "study" and words that differ only by morphological markers, such as "study" and "studies" are considered different words although they have a similar meaning. The traditional solution for improving their performance is to use more references. However, multiple references are rare and expensive. Moreover, these n-gram-based evaluations have been shown to be biased in favour of statistical methods, largely because they do not allow grammatically-costrained lexical freedom.

In recent years, many proposals have been put forth and new metrics have appeared and shown their good performance (Machacek and Bojar, 2013; Machacek and Bojar, 2014; Stanojević et al., 2015). However, improving the performance of existing metrics does not require developing a whole new metric. Proposals that modify existing metrics and show competitive results have also been proposed. One of the common solutions to improve traditional metrics consists in changing strict string matching to fuzzy matching at the surface level. For example, LeBLEU (Virpioja and Grönroos, 2015) — a variant of standard BLEU, also called "Letter-edit-BLEU" or "Levenshtein-BLEU" — takes into account letter-edit distance — Levenshtein distance including the spaces between the words — between hypothesis and references instead of strict n-gram matchings. More recently, Weiyue et al. (2016) have proposed a character-level TER (CharacTER) which calculates the character-level edit distance, while still performing the shift edits at the word level. The evaluation results show that this kind of modifications have a good effect on string-level similar words, but that they don't work well on words that are semantically similar, but are orthografically different strings.

To capture semantic similarity, one established way is to apply additional linguistic knowledge, such as synonym dictionaries. For example, TER-Plus (Snover et al., 2009) use WordNet (Fellbaum, 1998) to compute synonym matches in addition to the four original operations (Insertion, Deletion, Substitution and Shift). Although such linguistic resources are helpful, they are often lacking in coverage and affect computation speed and ease of use.

Current research on word embeddings (Bengio et al., 2003; Mikolov et al., 2013) maps each word to a low-dimensional vector. The vectors of the words that are semantically similar have been shown to be close to each other in vector space. The similarity between words then can be captured by calculating

33

Proceedings of the Sixth Workshop on Hybrid Approaches to Translation,
pages 33–41, Osaka, Japan, December 11, 2016.

the geometric distance between their vectors. On this basis, Le and Mikolov (2014) extend word-level representation to sentence and document level, which allows them to compute the similarity between two sequence of words. Recently, this kind of vector representation has been widely integrated in MT evaluation. Banchs et al. (2015) use Latent Semantic Indexing to project sentences as bag-of-words into a low-dimensional continuous space to measure the adequacy on an hypothesis. A monolingual continuous space has been used to capture the similarity between hypothesis and reference and a cross-language continuous space has been used to calculate the similarity between source sentence and hypothesis. With the same idea, Vela and Tan (2015) proposed a Bayesian Ridge Regressor which use document-level embeddings as features and METEOR score as target to predict the adequacy of hypothesis. The study of Chen and Guo (2015) uses vector representation more directly. In their study, each sentence has been transformed into a vector (they tried 3 kinds of vector representation: one-hot, word embedding and recursive auto-encoder representations). The evaluation score is calculated by the distance between the hypothesis vector and the reference vector, with a length penalty. More recently, Servan et al. (2016) combine word embeddings and DBnary (Sérasset, 2015), a multilingual lexical resource, to enrich ME-TEOR.

In this paper, we also incorporate word embeddings in our similarity score to improve machine translation evaluation metrics. We propose measures that, while being largely compatible with previous proposals (BLEU and WER), include semantic word similarity and improve on the state of the art. Differently from with the above-mentioned works, our approach simply uses monolingual word embeddings, and still has competitive performance at both sentence and system level.

Because these measures are modifications of BLEU and WER (we call them BLEU_{modif} and WER_{modif}), they also support systematic comparisons of results: if BLEU_{modif} or WER_{modif} is better correlated with human judgments because word embeddings allow it to better captures lexical semantic similarity, then the improvement in performance must be due to the fact that the system translation exhibits lexical semantic variation. These modified measures then allow us to compare different architectures according to their amount of lexical variation. Compared to the standard BLEU and WER versions, which have been argued to penalize rule-based systems more, these modified measures do not penalize systems based on their architecture. This gives us the possibility to evaluate fairly both the rule-based and the statistical components of a hybrid system.

In this paper, we will first descible our method in next section. Our experimental results in section 3 show that even a simple modification could significantly improve the performances over traditional metrics.

2 Method

The standard BLEU and WER metrics compute strict matching between n-grams or words. Our modifications for these two metrics is to use a similarity score between n-grams (words for WER) instead of strict matching. It has previously been shown that word embeddings represent the contextualised lexical semantics of words (Mikolov et al., 2013; Bengio et al., 2003). We first use the popular toolkit Word2Vec[1] provided by Mikolov et al. (2013) to train our word embeddings. At the word level, the similarity score between two words is the cosine similarity between word vectors. At the n-gram level, we average the vectors of all words in the n-gram and use the similarity between average vectors as the n-gram similarity score. All the Out-Of-Vocabulary words are skipped when computing the similarity score. For example, word vectors show that "study" and "studies" are very similar, while "study" and "play" are not very similar.

- Vector of "study" is [0.1049, -0.1103, ..., 0.0752]

- Vector of "studies" is [0.0035, -0.0799, ..., 0.1178]

- Vector of "play" is [-0.0250, 0.0531 ..., 0.0759]

- Similarity score of "study" and "studies": 0.534

---

[1] https://code.google.com/p/word2vec/

- Similarity score of "study" and "play": 0.058

Word2Vec provides two embedding algorithms, Skip-Gram and Continuous Bag-of-Words (CBOW). The study of Levy et al. (2015) and Mikolov et al. (2013) show that Skip-Gram better represents word similarity, but Baroni et al. (2014) show the opposite. In our study, we will use both of them, and try to find the better one for our modifications of BLEU and WER.

Our Python program uses the Gensim package[2] for implementing the trained word embeddings. The code of our modified measures is provided on the Github page[3] .

2.1 Modification for BLEU metric

The original BLEU score is calculated with the modified n-gram precision P_n and the brevity penalty BP, as shown in (1).

$$BLEU = BP \cdot exp(\sum_{n=1}^{N} w_n log P_n) \tag{1}$$

where w_n is a positive weight which is used to adjust the proportions of different n-grams. In the baseline of Papineni et al. (2002), they used $N = 4$ and uniform $w_n = 1/4$. The brevity penalty BP is used to penalise the translations that are shorter than their references.

The modified n-gram precision P_n is the proportion of matched n-grams ng between the translation sentence T and the corresponding reference sentence, shown in (2) and (3).

$$P_n = \frac{\sum_{ng \in T} C_{clip}(ng)}{\sum_{ng \in T} C(ng)} \tag{2}$$

$$C_{clip}(ng) = min\{C(ng), MaxC_{ref}(ng)\} \tag{3}$$

Here, $C_{clip}(ng)$ is called clipped counts, $MaxC_{ref}(ng)$ is the maximum value of the corresponding of matched n-gram in the reference.

One of BLEU's disadvantages is that the precision P_n considers a valid match only for those words that are identical between translations and references. We propose a modification for BLEU that instead of using the modified n-gram precision P_n uses the similarity n-gram precision P_{sim}, which is defined in (4).

$$P_{sim} = \frac{\sum_{ng \in T} Max_{sim_{pruned}}(ng, T, R, \gamma)}{\sum_{ng \in T} C(ng)} \tag{4}$$

In this formula, P_{sim} is computed as follows:

- Calculate the similarity scores between an n-gram(ng) in the translation sentence T and all the n-grams in the reference sentence R.

- Prune the maximum similarity score with a threshold γ.

- Sum the $Max_{sim_{pruned}}(ng, T, R, \gamma)$ of all the n-grams in T and divide the result by the the number of n-grams in T.

Our modified BLEU metric is defined in (5).

$$BLEU_{modif} = BP \cdot exp(\sum_{n=1}^{N} w_n log P_{sim}) \tag{5}$$

Same as Papineni et al. (2002), in our baseline, we use $N = 4$ and uniform $w_n = 1/4$. We will tune the threshold γ and try to find the best threshold.

---

[2] http://radimrehurek.com/gensim/index.html
[3] https://github.com/ChatonPatron/VecEval

2.2 Modification for WER metric

The standard word error rate is computed in the following way:

$$WER = \frac{S + D + I}{N} \tag{6}$$

where S is the number of substitutions, D is the number of deletions, I is the number of insertions and N is the number of words in the reference sentence. Normally, every action has a weight of 1, whether it is substitution, deletion or insertion. Assigning equal weights to all actions does not represent the intuition that the cost of a substitution depends on the similarity of the words. For example, if the cost of the needed operations is a measure of how hard it is to recover the real translation from the system translation, then the effort is not always the same, it depends on the quality of the translation. For example, if the translation word simply has a morphological error, the action "substitution" will be very easy, but if the translation word is completely different from the correct word, this action will be definitely harder. Our modification for the WER metric (WER_{modif}) focusses on the action "substitution": instead of giving the same weight to the three operations, we calculate their weights as shown in (7).

$$S_{modif} = 1 - Score_{sim}(word_{old}, word_{new}); D, I = 1 \tag{7}$$

Here, $Score_{sim}(word_{old}, word_{new})$ is the similarity score between the old word and the substituted word. Same with the standard WER, a higher score means a worse translation.

3 Experiments

We carried out some experiments to study our modified metrics. The experiments are based on the English-to-French, English-to-German and French-to-English, German-to-English data provided for the metrics task of the Workshops on Statistical Machine Translation (WMT) (Stanojević et al., 2015; Machacek and Bojar, 2014). This kind of data consists of human judgements for the outputs of different MT systems. The principle of the experiments is to tune and evaluate our modified metrics by measuring the correlation between our scores and the human judgement scores at the segment-level and at the system-level. The segment-level correlation is calculated by the Kendall's rank correlation coefficient and the system-level correlation is calculated by Pearson's correlation coefficient. We use the dataset of WMT-14[4] for the tuning task and WMT-15[5] for the evaluation task.

Our word embedding models are trained on a multilingual corpus called "News Crawl" shared by WMT-16[6]. This corpus contains a large amount of news articles from 2007 to 2015 in different languages. The size of our training data is 2.917 billion words for English, 0.877 billion words for French and 1.752 billion words for German. For each language, we trained two embedding models with the two different algorithms Skip-Gram (Vector Size = 500, Window Size = 10) and CBOW (Vector Size = 500, Window Size = 5)

3.1 Parameter Tuning

We first ran a grid search of ten values to tune the parameter γ (from $\gamma = 0.0$ to $\gamma = 0.9$) on the dataset of WMT-14. The results are reported in Figure 1. If we look at the figure of Skip-Grams (left), we find that the curves at the segment-level are very similar, the correlation score improves after $\gamma = 0.3$, but reduces quickly after $\gamma = 0.7$. The curves at the system level are quite different. For French,German-to-English, the correlation score gets a little improvement after $\gamma = 0.3$, but for English-to-French,German, the correlation score decreases directly after $\gamma = 0.3$. For the figure of CBOW, the curves are very similar. The correlation score stabilizes before $\gamma = 0.3$, and decreases after. Differently from Skip-gram, the correlation at the segment-level drops more quickly than the correlation at the system-level.

The tuning results reported in Table 1 give the numerical values of the best correlation scores. We can conclude that, for the modified BLEU measure ($BLEU_{modif}$), the best result at the segment-level (two

---

[4]http://www.statmt.org/wmt14/metrics-task/
[5]http://www.statmt.org/wmt15/metrics-task/
[6]http://www.statmt.org/wmt16/translation-task.html

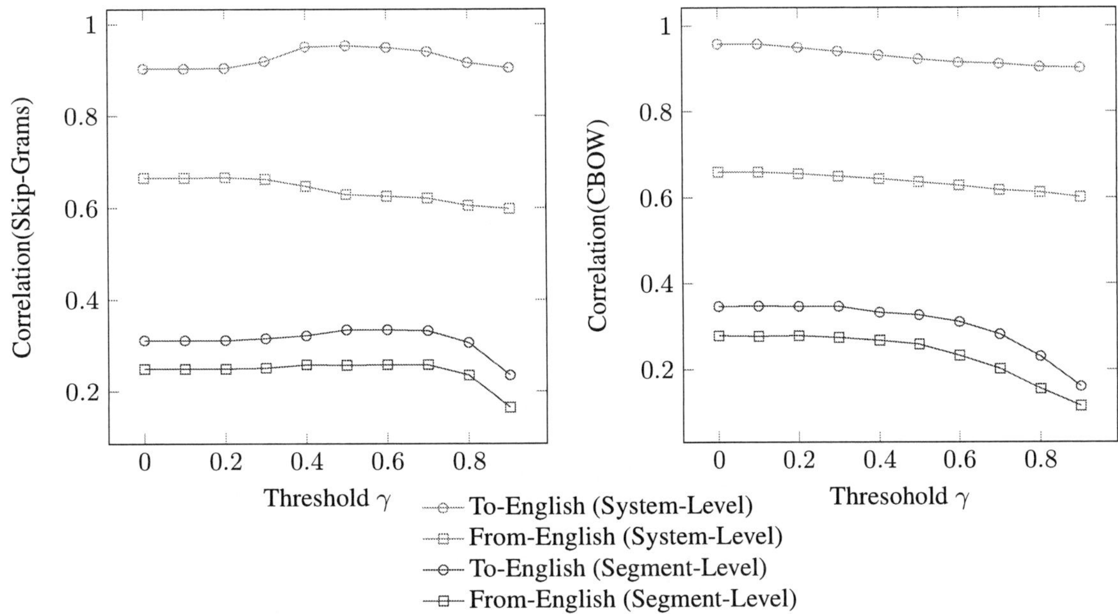

Figure 1: Results of tuning the threshold γ for modified BLEU on the WMT-14 dataset. To-En includes French and German to English. From-En includes English to French and German. The correlation scores are the averages of the two source (or target) languages. Note that in the WMT-14 metric task, all the results into German at the system-level are markedly lower than the others.

directions) and French,German-to-English at the system-level are produced by the CBOW algorithm with a threshold equal to 0.1. Skip-Gram with a threshold equal to 0.2 works best for the English-to-French,German system-level measure. For modified WER (WER_{modif}), CBOW always has a better result than Skip-Gram.

| | | Segment-Level | | | | System-Level | | | |
| | | To-En | | From-En | | To-En | | From-En | |
		Corr.	γ	Corr.	γ	Corr.	γ	Corr.	γ
BLEU_{modif}	Skip-Gram	0.335	0.6	0.259	0.5	0.954	0.5	**0.667**	0.2
	CBOW	**0.348**	0.1	**0.278**	0.1	**0.957**	0.1	0.660	0.1
WER_{modif}	Skip-Gram	0.332	-	0.253	-	0.942	-	0.662	-
	CBOW	**0.351**	-	**0.277**	-	**0.956**	-	**0.671**	-

Table 1: Tuning results: The results for modified BLEU shown in this table are the results of different embedding algorithms with the best threshold γ. To-En includes French and German to English. From-En includes English to French and German. The correlation scores are the averages of the languages mentioned.

3.2 Performance Evaluation

We evaluated our modified metrics on the dataset of WMT-15 with the best parameters found in the tuning phase. For a better understanding of the general performance of our measures, we compared our modified metrics with standard BLEU, sentence-level smoothed BLEU, TER, NIST and WER. The results reported in Table 2 show that, compared with their original versions, both the modified BLEU or the modified WER show an improvement on the correlation with human judgements, both at the segment-level and at the system-level. Their performance is much better than TER and NIST (Doddington, 2002), especially on the English-to-French,German data. If we observe the ranking of metrics, we find that

	Segment-Level				System-Level			
	To-En		From-En		To-En		From-En	
	Corr.	Rank	Corr.	Rank	Corr.	Rank	Corr.	Rank
Top	0.438	1/22	0.373	1/15	0.984	1/25	**0.922**	**1/18**
TER	-	-	-	-	0.935	20/25	0.756	13/18
NIST	-	-	-	-	0.941	17/25	0.726	15/18
BLEU	0.137	22/22	0.139	15/15	0.920	22/25	0.760	12/18
Sent-BLEU	0.359	19/22	0.306	13/15	-	-	-	-
BLEU_{modif}	**0.390**	14/22	**0.353**	7/15	**0.951**	13/25	**0.881**	7/18
WER	**0.373**	17/22	0.324	12/15	0.930	21/25	0.754	14/18
WER_{modif}	**0.397**	11/22	0.347	8/15	**0.949**	15/25	**0.922**	1/18

Table 2: System-level and segment-level correlation with the human judgement on the WMT-15 dataset. To-En includes French and German to English. From-En includes English to French and German. The correlation scores are the averages of the languages mentioned.

after our modifications, the ranks of BLEU and WER are increased by at least four or five ranks. For English-to-French,German system-level, the modified WER becomes the top metric among eighteenth participants.

The results show that a measure that simply augments matching by a similarity notion has better performance than strict string matching, and that current word embeddings techniques capture this notion of similarity.

	BLEU	BLEU_{modif}	WER	WER_{modif}
Hyp1:	0.508	0.835	0.333	0.178
Hyp2:	0.508	0.812	0.333	0.199
Hyp3:	0.508	0.797	0.333	0.219

Table 3: Single translation evaluation scores.

A qualitative analysis of results also shows that the captured notion of similarity corresponds to ranking of sentence alternatives by native speakers. For example, looking at some randomly chosen individual sentences, we find some interesting examples: The source sentence "History is a great teacher" is translated as "Die Geschichte ist ein großartiger Lehrmeister" in German. The following hypotheses are the output translations of three MT systems from WMT-15 translation task.

- Hypothesis 1: Die Geschichte ist ein guter Lehrer.

- Hypothesis 2: Die Geschichte ist ein großer Lehrer.

- Hypothesis 3: Die Geschichte ist ein großer Meister.

We used the original BLEU and WER and our modified versions to evaluate these three hypotheses. The scores are shown in Table 3. Before our modifications, the original BLEU and WER metrics give the same scores to these three different hypotheses. After our modifications, the modified measures are able to recognize the difference. According to a native German speaker, the rank of these hypotheses is : Hyp1>Hyp2>Hyp3. This rank is the same as what is proposed by the modified measures, showing that the measure is not only more accurate within a system, but also more sensitive to differences across systems.

When we observe the system-level scores of different participants of WMT-15 Translation Task, we find an interesting phenomenon. According to the human evaluation scores, for the English-to-German systems, the only Rule-based system "PROM-RULE" is ranked third among sixteen MT systems. The score of an online system "Online-A" is slightly lower but very close. According to the official report of the WMT-15 Translation Task (Bojar et al., 2015), these two systems are considered tied. However, if we re-rank all the systems by standard BLEU or WER, according to the results reported in Figure 2 and Table 4, we find that the rank of "PROM-RULE" decreases quickly from number three to number ten or eleven, and the rank of "Online-A" becomes much higher than "PROM-RULE". It is in fact well-known that because rule-based systems usually apply some dictionary resources, their lexical variation is richer than other kinds of MT systems. But this is the reason why these kinds of systems are usually considered good according to human judgements, but not as good when scored automatically. Our modifications changed the situation: we give the rule-based system the opportunity to score correctly by similar words. So that the rank of our modified metrics is similar to the rank of the human evaluation. Note that, for the modified BLEU, the scores are very close (the difference between the scores is less than 0.001), so that we can consider that, like the human judgements, they are at the same level.

	Human	BLEU	BLEU_{modif}	WER	WER_{modif}
PROM-RULE	0.2600	0.2253	0.7297	0.6887	0.5866
Online-A	0.2350	0.1859	0.7302	0.6284	0.5810

Table 4: English-to-German system-level evaluation scores of "PROM-RULE and "Online-A" (Systems from WMT-15 Translation Task)

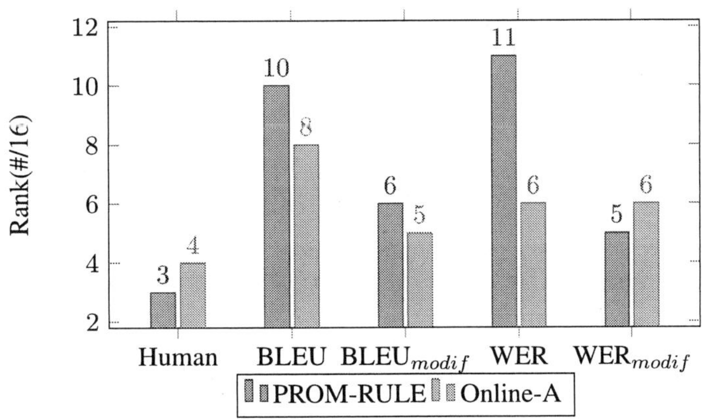

Figure 2: English-to-German system-level ranking of "PROM-RULE and "Online-A" (Systems from WMT-15 Translation Task)

4 Conclusions

In this paper, we have described our modifications for BLEU and WER metrics based on word-embeddings. The modifications allow these measures to take into account the semantic similarity of the words or of the n-grams, and not just string similarity. With this kind of semantic similarity, BLEU and WER do not penalize rule-based systems or rule-based components of hybrid systems more than statistical systems and lead to a fairer evaluation. Experiments on the WMT-15 metric task dataset shows that, compared to the standard BLEU and WER, the modified metrics obtains a better correlations with human judgments both at the segment-level and at the system-level. The improvement is quite apparent for the English-to-French,German data.

References

Rafael E Banchs, Luis F DHaro, and Haizhou Li. 2015. Adequacy–fluency metrics: Evaluating MT in the continuous space model framework. *IEEE/ACM Transactions on Audio, Speech, and Language Processing*, 23(3):472–482.

Marco Baroni, Georgiana Dinu, and Germán Kruszewski. 2014. Don't count, predict! A systematic comparison of context-counting vs. context-predicting semantic vectors. In *Proceedings of the 52nd Annual Meeting of the Association for Computational Linguistics*, pages 238–247, Baltimore, June.

Yoshua Bengio, Rejean Ducharme, Pascal Vincent, and Christian Jauvin. 2003. A Neural Probabilistic Language Model. *Journal of machine learning research*, 3:1137–1155.

Ondrej Bojar, Rajen Chatterjee, Christian Federmann, Barry Haddow, Matthias Huck, Chris Hokamp, Philipp Koehn, Varvara Logacheva, Christof Monz, Matteo Negri, Matt Post, Carolina Scarton, Lucia Specia, and Marco Turchi. 2015. Findings of the 2015 Workshop on Statistical Machine Translation. In *Proceedings of the Tenth Workshop on Statistical Machine Translation*, pages 1–46, Lisbon, Portugal, September.

Boxing Chen and Hongyu Guo. 2015. Representation-based Translation Evaluation Metrics. In *Proceedings of the 53rd Annual Meeting of the Association for Computational Linguistics and the 7th International Joint Conference on Natural Language Processing (Short Papers)*, pages 150–155, Beijing, July.

George Doddington. 2002. Automatic Evaluation of Machine Translation Quality Using N-gram Co-Occurrence Statistics. In *Proceedings of the Second International Conference on Human Language Technology Research*, pages 138–145, California, March.

Christiane Fellbaum. 1998. *WordNet: An Electronic Lexical Database*. The MIT Press, May.

Quoc Le and Tomas Mikolov. 2014. Distributed Representations of Sentences and Documents. In *Proceedings of The 31st International Conference on Machine Learning*, pages 1188–1196, Beijing, June.

Omer Levy, Yoav Goldberg, and Ido Dagan. 2015. Improving Distributional Similarity with Lessons Learned from Word Embeddings. *Transactions of the Association for Computational Linguistics*, 3:211–225, May.

Matouvs Machacek and Ondrej Bojar. 2013. Results of the WMT13 Metrics Shared Task. In *Proceedings of the Eighth Workshop on Statistical Machine Translation*, pages 45–51, Sofia, August.

Matouvs Machacek and Ondrej Bojar. 2014. Results of the WMT14 Metrics Shared Task. In *Proceedings of the Eighth Workshop on Statistical Machine Translation*, pages 293–301, Baltimore, June.

Tomas Mikolov, Ilya Sutskever, Chen Kai, Greg Corrado, and Jeffrey Dean. 2013. Distributed Representations of Words and Phrases and their Compositionality. *Advances in neural information processing systems*, pages 3111–3119.

Kishore Papineni, Salim Roukos, Todd Ward, and Wei-Jing Zhu. 2002. BLEU: a Method for Automatic Evaluation of Machine Translation. In *Proceedings of the Fortieth Annual Meeting of the Association for Computational Linguistics*, pages 311–318, Philadelphia, July.

Gilles Sérasset. 2015. DBnary: Wiktionary as a Lemon-based multilingual lexical resource in RDF. *Semantic Web*, 6(4):355–361.

Christophe Servan, Alexandre Bérard, Zied Elloumi, Hervé Blanchon, and Laurent Besacier. 2016. Word2Vec vs DBnary: Augmenting METEOR using Vector Representations or Lexical Resources? *arXiv preprint arXiv:1610.01291*.

Matthew G Snover, Bonnie Dorr, Richard Schwartz, Linnea Micciulla, and John Makhoul. 2006. A study of translation edit rate with targeted human annotation. In *Proceedings of Association for Machine Translation in the Americas*, volume 200, Boston, August.

Matthew G Snover, Nitin Madnani, Bonnie Dorr, and Richard Schwartz. 2009. Ter-plus: Paraphrase, semantic, and alignment enhancements to translation edit rate . *Machine Translation*, 23:117–127.

Miloš Stanojević, Amir Kamran, Philipp Koehn, and Ondrej Bojar. 2015. Results of the WMT15 Metrics Shared Task . In *Proceedings of the Tenth Workshop on Statistical Machine Translation*, pages 256–273, Lisbon, September.

Mihaela Vela and Liling Tan. 2015. Predicting Machine Translation Adequacy with Document Embeddings. In *Proceedings of the Tenth Workshop on Statistical Machine Translation (WMT)*, pages 402–410, Lisbon, September.

Sami Virpioja and Stig-Arne Grönroos. 2015. LeBLEU: N-gram-based Translation Evaluation Score for Morphologically Complex Languages. In *Proceedings of the Tenth Workshop on Statistical Machine Translation*, pages 411–416, Lisbon, September.

Wang Weiyue, Peter Jan-Thorsten, Rosendahl Hendrik, and Ney Hermann. 2016. CharacTER: Translation Edit Rate on Character Level. In *Proceedings of the First Conference on Machine Translation*, pages 505–510, Berlin, August.

Verb Sense Disambiguation in Machine Translation

Roman Sudarikov, Ondřej Dušek, Martin Holub, Ondřej Bojar, and **Vincent Kríž**
Charles University, Faculty of Mathematics and Physics
Institute of Formal and Applied Linguistics
{sudarikov,odusek,holub,bojar,kriz}@ufal.mff.cuni.cz

Abstract

We describe experiments in Machine Translation using word sense disambiguation (WSD) information. This work focuses on WSD in verbs, based on two different approaches – verbal patterns based on corpus pattern analysis and verbal word senses from valency frames. We evaluate several options of using verb senses in the source-language sentences as an additional factor for the Moses statistical machine translation system. Our results show a statistically significant translation quality improvement in terms of the BLEU metric for the valency frames approach, but in manual evaluation, both WSD methods bring improvements.

1 Introduction

The possibility of using word sense disambiguation (WSD) systems in machine translation (MT) has recently been investigated in several ways: Output of WSD systems has been incorporated into MT to improve translation quality — at the decoding step of a phrase-based statistical machine translation (PB-SMT) system (Chan et al., 2007) or as contextual features in maximum entropy (MaxEnt) models (Neale et al., 2015) and (Neale et al., 2016). In addition, WSD has also been used in MT evaluation, for example in METEOR (Apidianaki et al., 2015). These works indicate that WSD can be beneficial to different MT tasks, in case of using senses as contextual features for MaxEnt models Neale et al. (2016) achieve statistically significant improvement over the baseline for English-to-Portuguese translation. And Apidianaki et al. (2015) report that usage of WSD can establish better sense correspondences and improve its correlation with human judgments of translation quality.

In this research, we have investigated the possibilities of integrating two different approaches to verbal WSD into a PB-SMT system – verb patterns based on corpus pattern analysis (CPA) and verbal word senses in valency frames. The focus on verbs was motivated by the ideas that verbs carry a crucial part of the meaning of the sentence (Healy and Miller, 1970) and thus accurate translation of the verb is critical for the understanding of the translation. Therefore, improvement of the translation of verbs can lead to overall increase of the translation quality. Therefore, improvement of the translation of verbs can lead to an overall increase of translation quality. The outputs of automatic verb sense disambiguation systems using both CPA and valency frames were integrated into Moses statistical machine translation system(Koehn et al., 2007). Both kinds of verb senses were added as additional factors (Koehn and Hoang, 2007). Section 4.1 shows that we obtain statistically significant improvement in terms of BLEU scores (Papineni et al., 2002) and manual evaluation of translations validated that.

The novelty of this work lies not only in our focus only on verbs senses, but also in the fact that we are comparing the impact of two WSD approaches on the statistical machine translation.

The following Section 2 describes the initial setup of our experiments. Section 3 and Section 4 depict the idea behind corpus pattern analysis and verb valency frames representations and show evaluation results of incorporation of these sense to phrase-based statistical machine translation. The next section (Section 5) is devoted to the discussion of results obtained during the evaluation. And finally Section 6 describes our plan of the future work.

Proceedings of the Sixth Workshop on Hybrid Approaches to Translation,
pages 42–50, Osaka, Japan, December 11, 2016.

2 Experiments setup

2.1 Dataset and MT system

For our experiments, we have used a subset of the Czech-English corpus CzEng 1.0 (Bojar et al., 2012); the respective numbers of sentences and tokens in each of training, development and test sets are shown in Table 1. For our experiments, 28 different English verbs were selected and automatically annotated with corpus pattern analysis senses, and 3,306 verbs annotated using valency frames. The subset has been selected to include verbs annotated with CPA, so the effect of WSD would be visible. All the experiments were carried out in the Eman experiment management system (Bojar and Tamchyna, 2013) using the Moses PB-SMT system (Koehn et al., 2007) as the core and minimum error rate training (MERT, (Och, 2003)) to optimize the decoder feature weights on the development set. The evaluation was performed using the BLEU score (Papineni et al., 2002), but the results of each setup were then thoroughly examined and verified using the MT-ComparEval system (Aranberri et al., 2016)[1].

Set	Number of sentences	Tokens CS	Tokens EN
Training	649,605	10,759,546	12,073,130
Development	10,115	187,478	167,788
Test	2,707	59,446	67,336

Table 1: Data set composition

2.2 MT configurations

As we have mentioned in Section 1 the main goal of the experiments was to explore whether verb senses as additional factors in the statistical MT system Moses can help in improving translation quality. The following configurations were tested:

- Form→Form – "vanilla" Moses setup, translating from surface word forms to target surface forms, including capitalization.

- Form+Sense→Form – two source factors (surface word form and verb sense ID, if applicable) are translated to the target-side word forms. This is technically identical to appending the verb sense ID to the source words.

- Form→Form+Tag – the source word form is translated to two factors on the target side: word form and morphological tag (part-of-speech tag with morphological categories of Czech, such as case, number, gender, or tense). This allows us to use an additional language model trained on morphological tags only. This setup is known to perform well for morphologically rich languages (Bojar, 2007) and thus was selected as a baseline for all comparisons.

- Form+Sense→Form+Tag – a combination of the two setups above: two source and two target-side factors, for better handling of source verb meaning and target morphological coherence.

- Form→Form+Tag + Form+Sense→Form+Tag – a combination of previous two models as two separate phrase tables.

For all configurations, we trained a 4-gram language model on word forms of the sentences from the training set. This LM was pruned: we discarded all singleton n-grams (apart from unigrams). In addition, for configurations which generated morphological tags, we used a 10-gram model LM over morphological tags to help maintain morphological coherence of the translation outputs. Again, we pruned all singleton n-grams with the exception of unigrams.

---

[1] http://wmt.ufal.cz/

Verb	No.	Pattern / Implicature
gleam	1	**[[Physical Object | Surface]] gleam [NO OBJ]** [[Surface]] of [[Physical Object]] reflects occasional flashes of light
gleam	2	**[[Light | Light Source]] gleam [NO OBJ]** [[Light Source]] emits an occasional flash of [[Light]]
gleam	3	**{eyes} gleam [NO OBJ] (with [[Emotion]])** {eyes} of [[Human]] shine, expressive of [[Emotion]]
wake	3	**[no object] [Human] wake ({up}) AdvTime({from} {nightmare | dream | sleep | reverie}) ({to} Eventuality)** the mind of [[Human]] returns at a particular [[Time]] to a state of full conscious awareness and alertness after sleep
wake	4	**pv [phrasal verb] [[Human 1] ̂ [Sound] ̂ [Event]] wake [[Human 2] ̂ [Animal]] ({up})** [[Human 1 — Sound — Event]] causes the mind of [[Human 2 — Animal]] to return to a state of full conscious awareness and alertness after sleep
wake	7	**[Anything] wake [Emotion] ({in} Human)** [[Anything]] causes [[Human]] to feel or become aware of [[Emotion]]
wake	9	**waking * ({up})** [Human—Animal]'s returning to a state of full conscious awareness and alertness after sleep

Table 2: Example patterns defined for the verbs *gleam* and *wake*.

3 Verb patterns based on Corpus Pattern Analysis

Corpus Pattern Analysis (CPA) is a method of manual context-based lexical disambiguation of verbs (Hanks, 1994; Hanks, 2013). Verbs are supposed to have no meanings on their own; instead, meanings are triggered by the context. Hence, a CPA-based lexicon does not group the uses of a verb into senses but into syntagmatic usage patterns derived from the corpus findings. Such a CPA-based lexicon is the Pattern Lexicon of English Verbs (PDEV, (Hanks and Pustejovsky, 2005)). In contrast to the classical WSD, here the verb patterns are used as verb meaning representations. An example of a few patterns is given in Table 2.

Here we employ an automatic procedure for verb pattern recognition developed by Holub et al. (2012), which deals with 30 selected English verbs. In fact, their method uses 30 separate classifiers, one for each verb, trained on moderately sized manually annotated samples. They use the collection called VPS-30-En (Verb Pattern Sample, 30 English verbs) published by Cinková et al. (2012) as training data. VPS-30-En was designed as a small sample of PDEV, a pilot lexical resource of 30 English lexical verb entries enriched with semantically annotated corpus samples. The data describes regular contextual patterns of use of the selected verbs in the British National Corpus, version 3 (BNC, 2007).[2] The number of different patterns varies from 4 to 10 in most cases across the verbs, and the performance of Holub et al. (2012)'s automatic pattern recognition also differs verb from verb, ranging between 50% and 90% accuracy.

3.1 Experiments and evaluation

For the experiments with verb patterns based on CPA, we have explored all the configurations described in Section 2.2.

Table 3 shows the results of the best MERT run for each configuration. Multiple MERT runs evaluation was performed for Form→Form+Tag, Form+Sense→Form+Tag, and Form→Form+Tag + Form+Sense→Form+Tag using MultEval system (Clark et al., 2011) with Form→Form+Tag as the baseline system, and the results are shown in Table 4. We see that the average results of Form+Sense→Form+Tag are worse than the ones of Form→Form+Tag by 0.1% BLEU. MultEval aims to determine whether an experimental result has a statistically reliable difference for a give evaluation metric, using a stratified approximate randomization (AR) test. AR estimates the probability (p-value) that a measured difference in metric scores arose by chance by randomly exchanging sentences between the two systems. If there is no significant difference between the systems (i.e., the null hypothesis is true), then this shuffling should not change the computed metric score (Clark et al., 2011). While comparing

---

[2]Details about both selected verbs and training contexts can be found at `http://ufal.mff.cuni.cz/spr`.

Configuration	BLEU
Form→Form	24.26
Form+Sense→Form	24.15
Form+Sense→Form+Tag	25.01
Form→Form+Tag	25.11
Form→Form+Tag + Form+Sense→Form+Tag	25.27

Table 3: Evaluation results for corpus pattern analysis annotation, best MERT run

Form→Form+Tag and Form→Form+Tag + Form+Sense→Form+Tag, we see that p-value is 0.16, thus allowing us to claim, that these two systems don't differ one from another. The same test performed using METEOR and TER tests only confirms that (in case of TER having p-value=0.61).

Metric	System	Avg	$\overline{s}_{\text{sel}}$	s_{Test}	p-value
BLEU	Form→Form+Tag	25.0	0.9	0.1	-
	Form+Sense→Form+Tag	24.9	0.9	0.1	0.00
	Form→Form+Tag + Form+Sense→Form+Tag	25.0	0.9	0.1	0.16
METEOR	Form→Form+Tag	22.6	0.4	0.0	-
	Form+Sense→Form+Tag	22.5	0.4	0.0	0.00
	Form→Form+Tag + Form+Sense→Form+Tag	22.6	0.4	0.1	0.22
TER	Form→Form+Tag	62.2	0.7	0.2	-
	Form+Sense→Form+Tag	62.4	0.7	0.1	0.00
	Form→Form+Tag + Form+Sense→Form+Tag	62.2	0.7	0.2	0.61

Table 4: Multeval results for corpus pattern analysis, based on 36 MERT runs

We also performed a more detailed analysis with pairwise comparisons of the following configurations:

- Form→Form vs. Form+Sense→Form

- Form→Form+Tag vs. Form+Sense→Form+Tag

- Form→Form+Tag vs. Form→Form+Tag + Form+Sense→Form+Tag

3.1.1 Form→Form vs. Form+Sense→Form

The comparison provided by MT-ComparEval based on paired bootstrap resampling (Koehn, 2004) of best MERT runs for both configurations showed that Form→Form is significantly better (p-value=0.022) than Form+Sense→Form. The sentence-by-sentence comparison explains this: On the positive side, 8 examples out of the top 10 sentences where Form+Sense→Form output was better than Form→Form profited from using additional information about the verb sense. On the negative side, the model with verb senses made a lot of errors due to badly extracted phrase tables, even leaving some verbs untranslated.

3.1.2 Form→Form+Tag vs. Form+Sense→Form+Tag

In this case the same paired bootstrap resampling of the best MERT runs showed that the difference between Form+Sense→Form+Tag and Form→Form+Tag outputs is not significant (p-value=0.062). In the sentence by sentence comparison, we saw that while information about verb pattern helps to deal with some translations, it still causes mistakes.

For example, in the sentence from Figure 1, the verb *cool down* is translated as *vychladnout* ('let the temperature sink') instead of the correct *uklidnit* ('calm down'). Here, MT-ComparEval shows that Form→Form+Tag translated the verb correctly, meaning that the correct translation exists in the training data. Therefore, we checked which of the translation model factors caused the wrong translation. In the source sentence, the verb *cool* has the CPA pattern "1", but the only suitable phrase in the Form+Sense→Form+Tag phrase table (with `cool|1 down|-` on the source side) has the verb *vychladnout* on the target side. In the Form→Form+Tag table, we have the phrase `cool down and let` translated using the verb *uklidnit*, but the corresponding phrase in the Form+Sense→Form+Tag table has has a different CPA pattern "u" for the verb *cool*.

Source	You cool down and let me handle this !
Reference	Co , kdyby ses uklidnil a nechal to na mě ?
FromVerb_FromTag	Ty vychladnout a nech mě jednat !
Form_FormTag	Člověk se uklidnil a nechal mě jednat !

Figure 1: An example MT-ComparEval output from the Form+Sense→Form+Tag sentence analysis

work[1]: ACT PAT DIR3
(put, implement)
Burger King works a sales pitch into its public-service message.
work[2]: ACT ?PAT ?BEN ?ACMP
(perform a job)
Mr. Cray has been working on the project for more than six years.
work[3]: ACT PAT
(cause, create)
[. . .] greenhouse effect that will work important climatic changes [. . .]
work[4]: ACT
(function)
US trade law is working.

Figure 2: Example entry from the EngVallex valency dictionary, with four different senses/valency frames of the verb *work* (abridged, with minor adaptations for presentation).

The sense ID and the valency frame is shown on the 1st line of each sense, with the following semantic roles: ACT = actor, PAT = patient, DIR3 = direction (to, into), BEN = benefactor, ACMP = accompanying person or object. Optional arguments are prepended with a "?". A short gloss is shown on the 2nd line, and an example on the 3rd line.

3.1.3 Form→Form+Tag vs. Form→Form+Tag + Form+Sense→Form+Tag

The MT-ComparEval's paired bootstrap resampling showed that the difference between these two outputs is significant (p-value=0.023), thus showing that output of Form→Form+Tag + Form+Sense→Form+Tag is significantly better than Form→Form+Tag. In the sentence-by-sentence comparison, we saw that the combined system benefited from the verb patterns where possible but resorted to the more general translation of the baseline phrase-table when CPA-annotated translations were insufficient.

4 Verbal word senses in valency frames

Valency in verbs (and other parts of speech), i.e., the ability of a verb to require and shape its arguments, is one of the core notions of the Functional Generative Description (FGD) theory (Sgall et al., 1986). The valency of a verb is described in a valency frame, which lists the semantic roles and possible syntactic shapes of all of its obligatory and optional arguments. Since different senses of the same verb require different arguments and thus are described by different valency frames, this amounts to WSD in verbs (an example is shown in Figure 2).

Valency frames for over 7,000 senses of more than 4,000 common English verbs are listed in the Eng-Vallex valency lexicon (Cinková, 2006),[3] and the Prague Czech-English Dependency Treebank (PCEDT) 2.0 (Hajič et al., 2012) provides manually annotated valency frame IDs for all of its verbs. Using this annotation, Dušek et al. (2015) trained an automatic system for valency frame detection as a part of the Treex natural language processing toolkit (Popel and Žabokrtský, 2010).[4] We processed all the sentences in our dataset with the tool and used the resulting valency frame IDs in our experiments.

4.1 Experiments and evaluation

Based on the results of the experiments shown in Section 3.1, we have decided to focus only on the following configurations: Form→Form+Tag, Form+Sense→Form+Tag and their combination

---

[3]EngVallex is origially based on the PropBank frame files (Palmer et al., 2005), but it also contains a lot of manual changes.
[4]http://ufal.mff.cuni.cz/treex

Configuration	BLEU
Form+Sense→Form+Tag	24.97
Form→Form+Tag	25.08
Form→Form+Tag + Form+Sense→Form+Tag	25.26

Table 5: Evaluation results for valency frames annotation, best MERT for each configuration

Form→Form+Tag + Form+Sense→Form+Tag.

Table 5 shows the results for best MERT runs for each configuration. MultEval MERT evaluation for the all configurations mentioned above, with Form→Form+Tag as a baseline, is shown in Table 6. The table shows that the average Form+Sense→Form+Tag model results are still 0.1% BLEU worse than the Form→Form+Tag model, but the average results of the combined Form→Form+Tag + Form+Sense→Form+Tag model are 0.1% BLEU better than the average results of Form→Form+Tag. The results of MultEval's stratified approximate randomization test (Clark et al., 2011) allow us to claim that the combination of these two models is statistically significantly better than the baseline. The same is true for METEOR and TER tests results, shown in the same table. It also shows that the valency frames approach to WSD has more impact on MT than CPA in our case.

Metric	System	Avg	$\bar{s}_{sel}$	s_{Test}	*p*-value
BLEU	Form→Form+Tag	25.0	0.9	0.1	-
	Form+Sense→Form+Tag	24.9	0.9	0.1	0.01
	Form→Form+Tag + Form+Sense→Form+Tag	25.1	0.9	0.1	0.00
METEOR	Form→Form+Tag	22.5	0.4	0.0	-
	Form+Sense→Form+Tag	22.5	0.4	0.0	0.01
	Form→Form+Tag + Form+Sense→Form+Tag	22.6	0.4	0.0	0.00
TER	Form→Form+Tag	62.2	0.7	0.1	-
	Form+Sense→Form+Tag	62.4	0.7	0.2	0.00
	Form→Form+Tag + Form+Sense→Form+Tag	62.1	0.7	0.2	0.00

Table 6: MultEval results for valency frames, based on 8 MERT runs

A more thorough examination of the best MERT runs of following pairs of configurations in MT-ComparEval output of paired bootstrap resampling showed that:

- Form+Sense→Form+Tag is insignificantly worse than Form→Form+Tag, with p-value=0.0161

- Form→Form+Tag + Form+Sense→Form+Tag is significantly better than Form→Form+Tag, with p-value=0.002

An interesting observation was that Form+Sense→Form+Tag and Form→Form+Tag + Form+Sense→Form+Tag models were more likely to translate verbs as verbs, while translation errors in Form→Form+Tag often were caused by its efforts to translate verbs as nouns.

4.2 Comparsion of CPA and valency frames

Based on the MultEval results shown in Table 4 and Table 6, it can be claimed that using the valency frames approach to WSD helped to achieve a statistically significant improvement in machine translation, while CPA did not help to such an extent. Among the possible reasons are a lower number of verbs covered (for the same number of sentences, we had CPA-based annotations only for 28 different verbs and 3,306 different verbs with valency frames annotations) and the precision of automatic annotating system itself. One of the future plans here is to compare the results of these approaches when exactly the same verbs are annotated.

An example of the sentence where the valency frames approach was more successful than CPA is "…forged steel components for the automotive industry". Here, the word *forged* was annotated by verbal valency frame and by verbal pattern, and while valency frame provided correct translation of this word into Czech "*kované* oceli součástí", the CPA-based model generated "*zfalšoval* ocel součástí", which is incorrect in both the meaning and the part of speech.

5 Discussion and conclusion

Including verb senses – be it based on corpus pattern analysis or as valency frames – as an additional factor to a PB-SMT English-to-Czech model did not help by itself, as our results for Form+Sense→Form+Tag configurations have shown. Nevertheless, the combination of this model with a better-performing model Form→Form+Tag resulted in a significant improvement for the case of using senses based on valency frames, as shown by paired boootstrap resampling tests given in Table 6, while a manual evaluation of best MERT runs showed translation quality improvement for both WSD approaches. All the results were achieved on a relatively small data sets, but it can be of use in cases when one does not have enough parallel data, but WSD for the source language (which is often English) is available, for example, in case of domain-specific translations.

We have tried to use sense information produced by two different approaches to verbal WSD disambiguation – corpus pattern analysis and valency frames – and while the former did not significantly outperform the baseline system in terms of the BLEU metric, the later showed significant improvement.

Adding the automatic WSD system as additional preprocessing layer can influence the SMT system due to the fact that WSD system cannot deliver 100% accurate senses, thus causing confusing situations, when the system had a correct translation available, but did not select it because the verb sense of the source sentence from test set was incorrect. Possible ways of reducing the impact of such things are improvement of automatic WSD systems used and using WSD system combination.

6 Future work

In the future, we plan to continue our experiments on verbs senses using approached described in this work as well as other approaches, e.g. WSD systems based on BabelNet synsets (Navigli and Ponzetto, 2012) and WordNet senses.[5] In addition, we are going to experiment with the size of the corpus used for training, because this research used only a part of available Czech-English parallel corpus.

7 Acknowledgments

This research was supported by the grants H2020-ICT-2014-1-645452, GBP103/12/G084, SVV 260 333, and using language resources distributed by the LINDAT/CLARIN project of the Ministry of Education, Youth and Sports of the Czech Republic (LM2015071). We thank the two anonymous reviewers for useful comments.

References

Marianna Apidianaki, Benjamin Marie, and Lingua et Machina. 2015. METEOR-WSD: improved sense matching in MT evaluation. *Syntax, Semantics and Structure in Statistical Translation*, page 49.

Nora Aranberri, Eleftherios Avramidis, Aljoscha Burchardt, Ondrej Klejch, Martin Popel, and Maja Popovic. 2016. Tools and guidelines for principled machine translation development. In *Proceedings of the Tenth International Conference on Language Resources and Evaluation (LREC 2016)*, pages 1877–1882, Portorož, Slovenia.

BNC. 2007. British national corpus, version 3 (BNC XML edition). Distributed by Oxford University Computing Services on behalf of the BNC Consortium. URL: http://www.natcorp.ox.ac.uk/.

Ondřej Bojar and Aleš Tamchyna. 2013. The Design of Eman, an Experiment Manager. *The Prague Bulletin of Mathematical Linguistics*, 99:39–58.

Ondřej Bojar, Zdeněk Žabokrtský, Ondřej Dušek, Petra Galuščáková, Martin Majliš, David Mareček, Jiří Maršík, Michal Novák, Martin Popel, and Aleš Tamchyna. 2012. The Joy of Parallelism with CzEng 1.0. In *Proceedings of LREC 2012*, Istanbul, Turkey, May. ELRA, European Language Resources Association. In print.

Ondřej Bojar. 2007. English-to-Czech Factored Machine Translation. In *Proceedings of the Second Workshop on Statistical Machine Translation*, pages 232–239, Prague, Czech Republic, June. Association for Computational Linguistics.

---

[5] http://wordnet.princeton.edu

Yee Seng Chan, Hwee Tou Ng, and David Chiang. 2007. Word sense disambiguation improves statistical machine translation. In *Proceedings of the 45th Annual Meeting of the Association for Computational Linguistics*, pages 33–40, Prague, Czech Republic.

Silvie Cinková, Martin Holub, Adam Rambousek, and Lenka Smejkalová. 2012. A database of semantic clusters of verb usages. In *Proceedings of the LREC 2012 International Conference on Language Resources and Evaluation*. Istanbul, Turkey.

Silvie Cinková. 2006. From PropBank to EngValLex: Adapting the PropBank-Lexicon to the Valency Theory of the Functional Generative Description. In *Proceedings of the fifth International conference on Language Resources and Evaluation (LREC 2006), Genova, Italy*.

Jonathan H Clark, Chris Dyer, Alon Lavie, and Noah A Smith. 2011. Better hypothesis testing for statistical machine translation: Controlling for optimizer instability. In *Proceedings of the 49th Annual Meeting of the Association for Computational Linguistics: Human Language Technologies: short papers-Volume 2*, pages 176–181. Association for Computational Linguistics.

Ondřej Dušek, Eva Fučíková, Jan Hajič, Martin Popel, Jana Šindlerová, and Zdeňka Urešová. 2015. Using Parallel Texts and Lexicons for Verbal Word Sense Disambiguation. In *Proceedings of the Third International Conference on Dependency Linguistics (Depling 2015)*, pages 82–90, Uppsala, Sweden.

J. Hajič, E. Hajičová, J. Panevová, P. Sgall, O. Bojar, S. Cinková, E. Fučíková, M. Mikulová, P. Pajas, J. Popelka, J. Semecký, J. Šindlerová, J. Štěpánek, J. Toman, Z. Urešová, and Z. Žabokrtský. 2012. Announcing Prague Czech-English Dependency Treebank 2.0. In *Proceedings of LREC*, pages 3153–3160, Istanbul.

Patrick Hanks and James Pustejovsky. 2005. A Pattern Dictionary for Natural Language Processing. *Revue Francaise de linguistique appliquée*, 10(2).

Patrick Hanks. 1994. Linguistic norms and pragmatic exploitations, or why lexicographers need prototype theory and vice versa. In F. Kiefer, G. Kiss, and J. Pajzs, editors, *Papers in Computational Lexicography: Complex '94*. Research Institute for Linguistics, Hungarian Academy of Sciences.

Patrick Hanks. 2013. *Lexical Analysis: Norms and Exploitations*. University Press Group Limited.

Alice F Healy and George A Miller. 1970. Verb as main determinant of sentence meaning. *Psychonomic Science*, 20(6):372–372.

Martin Holub, Vincent Kríz, Silvie Cinková, and Eckhard Bick. 2012. Tailored feature extraction for lexical disambiguation of english verbs based on corpus pattern analysis. In *COLING*, pages 1195–1210.

Philipp Koehn and Hieu Hoang. 2007. Factored Translation Models. In *Proc. of EMNLP*.

Philipp Koehn, Hieu Hoang, Alexandra Birch, Chris Callison-Burch, Marcello Federico, Nicola Bertoldi, Brooke Cowan, Wade Shen, Christine Moran, Richard Zens, Chris Dyer, Ondřej Bojar, Alexandra Constantin, and Evan Herbst. 2007. Moses: Open source toolkit for statistical machine translation. In *Proceedings of the annual meeting of the Association for Computational Linguistics*, pages 187–193.

Philipp Koehn. 2004. Statistical significance tests for machine translation evaluation. In *EMNLP*, pages 388–395. Citeseer.

Roberto Navigli and Simone Paolo Ponzetto. 2012. BabelNet: The automatic construction, evaluation and application of a wide-coverage multilingual semantic network. *Artificial Intelligence*, 193:217–250.

Steven Neale, Luıs Gomes, and António Branco. 2015. First steps in using word senses as contextual features in maxent models for machine translation. In *1st Deep Machine Translation Workshop*, page 64.

Steven Neale, Luıs Gomes, Eneko Agirre, Oier Lopez de Lacalle, and António Branco. 2016. Word sense-aware machine translation: Including senses as contextual features for improved translation models. In *Proceedings of the Tenth International Conference on Language Resources and Evaluation (LREC 2016)*, pages 2777–2783, Portorož, Slovenia.

Franz Josef Och. 2003. Minimum error rate training in statistical machine translation. In *Proceedings of the 41st Annual Meeting on Association for Computational Linguistics-Volume 1*, pages 160–167.

Martha Palmer, Daniel Gildea, and Paul Kingsbury. 2005. The proposition bank: An annotated corpus of semantic roles. *Computational Linguistics*, 31(1):71–106.

Kishore Papineni, Salim Roukos, Todd Ward, and Wei-Jing Zhu. 2002. BLEU: a method for automatic evaluation of machine translation. In *Proceedings of the 40th annual meeting of the Association for Computational Linguistics*, pages 311–318.

Martin Popel and Zdeněk Žabokrtský. 2010. TectoMT: modular NLP framework. In *Proceedings of IceTAL, 7th International Conference on Natural Language Processing*, pages 293–304, Reykjavík.

P. Sgall, E. Hajičová, and J. Panevová. 1986. *The meaning of the sentence in its semantic and pragmatic aspects.* D. Reidel, Dordrecht.

Improving word alignment for low resource languages using English monolingual SRL

Meriem Beloucif, Markus Saers and Dekai Wu
Human Language Technology Center
Department of Computer Science and Engineering
Hong Kong University of Science and Technology
`{mbeloucif|masaers|dekai}@cs.ust.hk`

Abstract

We introduce a new statistical machine translation approach specifically geared to learning translation from low resource languages, that exploits monolingual English semantic parsing to bias inversion transduction grammar (ITG) induction. We show that in contrast to conventional statistical machine translation (SMT) training methods, which rely heavily on phrase memorization, our approach focuses on learning bilingual correlations that help translating low resource languages, by using the output language semantic structure to further narrow down ITG constraints. This approach is motivated by previous research which has shown that injecting a semantic frame based objective function while training SMT models improves the translation quality. We show that including a monolingual semantic objective function during the learning of the translation model leads towards a semantically driven alignment which is more efficient than simply tuning loglinear mixture weights against a semantic frame based evaluation metric in the final stage of statistical machine translation training. We test our approach with three different language pairs and demonstrate that our model biases the learning towards more semantically correct alignments. Both GIZA++ and ITG based techniques fail to capture meaningful bilingual constituents, which is required when trying to learn translation models for low resource languages. In contrast, our proposed model not only improve translation by injecting a monolingual objective function to learn bilingual correlations during early training of the translation model, but also helps to learn more meaningful correlations with a relatively small data set, leading to a better alignment compared to either conventional ITG or traditional GIZA++ based approaches.

1 Introduction

In this paper we introduce a new approach for inversion transduction grammar (ITG) induction for low resource languages. Our induction algorithm uses the output language (English) semantic frames. Recent research showed that including a semantic frame based objective function at an early stage of training statistical machine translation (SMT) systems helps to learn more meaningful word alignments (Beloucif et al., 2015) rather than relying on tuning against a semantic based objective function such as MEANT (Lo et al., 2012), which improves the translation adequacy (Lo et al., 2013a; Lo and Wu, 2013a; Lo et al., 2013b; Beloucif et al., 2014). We show that integrating a semantic based objective function much earlier in the training pipeline not only helps to learn more semantically correct alignments, but also helps us get rid of the heavy memorization used in conventional training methods, which is paramount for low resource languages where data sparseness makes memorization ineffective.

Our approach is also motivated by the fact that inversion transduction grammar alignments have previously been empirically shown to cover 100% of crosslingual semantic frame alternations, while ruling out the majority of incorrect alignments (Addanki et al., 2012). We experiment on three different language pairs from the DARPA LORELEI study on efficient learning under low resource conditions: Chinese, Hausa, Uzbek, always translating into English.

We show that integrating a semantic frame based objective function much earlier in the training pipeline not only produces more semantically correct alignments but also helps to learn bilingual correlations without memorizing from a huge amount of parallel corpora. We believe that low resource conditions are

Proceedings of the Sixth Workshop on Hybrid Approaches to Translation,
pages 51–60, Osaka, Japan, December 11, 2016.

more interesting than high resource conditions because they are both scientifically and socioeconomically more interesting as they emphasize issues of efficient generalization as opposed to mere memorization from big data collections. We report results and examples showing that this way for inducing ITGs gives better translation quality compared to the conventional ITG (Saers and Wu, 2009) and GIZA++ (Och and Ney, 2000) alignments.

2   Related work

2.1   Alignment

Word alignment is considered to be an important step in training machine translation systems, since it helps to learn the correlations between the input and the output languages. Unfortunately, conventional alignments are generally based on training IBM models (Brown *et al.*, 1990), which are known to produce weak word alignment since they allow unstructured movement of words. Then use heuristics to combine alignments of both directions to produce the final alignment. A hidden Markov model (HMM) based alignment was proposed (Vogel *et al.*, 1996), but similarly to IBM models, the objective function uses surface based alignment rather than a more structure based alignment. No constraints are used while training, allowing any random word-to-word permutations. Such an alignment generally hurts the translation accuracy. The traditional GIZA++ (Och and Ney, 2000) toolkit implements both IBM and HMM models described above.

Saers and Wu (2009) proposed a better method of producing word alignment by training inversion transduction grammars (Wu, 1997). One problem encountered with such a model was the exhaustive biparsing that runs in $O(n^6)$. A more efficient version that runs in $O(n^3)$ was proposed later (Saers *et al.*, 2009).

Zens and Ney (2003) show that ITG constraints allow a higher flexibility in word ordering for longer sentences than the conventional IBM model. Furthermore, they demonstrate that applying ITG constraints for word alignment leads to learning a significantly better alignment than the constraints used in conventional IBM models for both German-English and French-English. Zhang and Gildea (2005) presented a version of ITG where rule probabilities are lexicalized throughout the synchronous parse tree for efficient training which helped to align sentences up to 15 words.

Some of the previous work on word alignment used morphological and syntactic features (De Gispert *et al.*, 2006). Some loglinear models have been proposed to incorporate those features (Dyer *et al.*, 2011). The problem with those approaches is that they require language specific knowledge and that they work better on more morphologically rich languages.

Few studies that approximately integrate semantic knowledge in computing word alignment are proposed by Ma *et al.* (2011) and Songyot and Chiang (2014). However, the former needs to have a prior word alignment learned on lexical words. The authors in the latter model proposed a semantic oriented word alignment. However, the problem is, they need to extract word similarity from the monolingual data for both languages, which is problematic in low resource conditions, then produce alignments using word similarities.

2.2   Inversion transduction grammars

Inversion transduction grammars, or ITGs, (Wu, 1997) are by definition a subset of syntax-directed transduction grammar (Lewis and Stearns, 1968; Aho and Ullman, 1972). A transduction is a set of bisentences that define the relation between an input language L_0 and an output language L_1. Accordingly, transduction grammars are able to:

$$\begin{cases} generate & (e, f \mid S) \\[2mm] translate & (e \mid f, S) \text{ or } (f \mid e, S) \\[2mm] accept & (S \mid e, f) \end{cases} \qquad (1)$$

Table 1: The size of the different data sets in sentence pairs (foreign-English).

	Uzbek	Hausa	Chinese
Training	148,190	76,910	39,953
Development	1,200	1,000	1,512
Test	600	500	489

where (e, f) is a sentence pair in L_0 and L_1 and S is the start symbol. Inversion transductions are syntax-directed transductions generated by inversion transduction grammars.

An ITG can always be written in a 2-normal form. Representing the ITG as a tuple $\langle N, V_0, V_1, R, S \rangle$ where N is a set of nonterminals, V_0 and V_1 are the tokens of L_0 and L_1 respectively, R is a set of transduction rules and $S \in N$ is the start symbol, each transduction rule can be restricted to one of the following forms:

$$S \to A$$
$$A \to [BC]$$
$$A \to \langle BC \rangle$$
$$A \to e/\epsilon$$
$$A \to \epsilon/f$$
$$A \to e/f$$

where S, A, B, C are the non-terminals, e, f are tokens in the two languages and ϵ is the empty token.

ITGs allow both straight and inverted rules, straight transduction rules use square brackets and take the form $A \to [BC]$ and inverted rules use inverted brackets and take the form $A \to \langle BC \rangle$. Straight transduction rules generate transductions with the same order in L_0 and L_1, inverted rules on the other hand, generate transduction in an inverted order. This means that, in the parse tree, the children instantiated by straight rules are read in the same order and children instantiated in an inverted order are read in an inverted order in L_1.

The rule probability function p is initialized using uniform probabilities for the structural rules, and a translation table t that is trained using IBM model 1 (Brown *et al.*, 1993) in both directions.

There are also many ways to formulate the model over ITGs: Wu (1995); Zhang and Gildea (2005); Chiang (2007); Cherry and Lin (2007); Blunsom *et al.* (2009); Haghighi *et al.* (2009); Saers *et al.* (2010); Neubig *et al.* (2011).

In this work, we use BITGs or bracketing transduction grammars (Saers *et al.*, 2009) which only use one single nonterminal category and surprisingly achieve good results.

2.3 Semantic frames in the MT training pipeline

Semantic role labeling (SRL) is an important task in natural language processing since it helps to define the basic event structure in a given sentence: *who did what to whom, for whom, when, where, how* and *why* as defined in (Pradhan *et al.*, 2004; Lo and Wu, 2011, 2012; Lo *et al.*, 2012). This approach gives a better way of understanding the meaning of a given sentence than the conventional syntax-based parsing.

Recent approaches in semantic role labeling use unsupervised machine learning techniques to automatically find the semantic roles. They generally use FrameNet (Gildea and Jurafsky, 2002) or Proposition Bank (Palmer *et al.*, 2005) notation to specify what a predicate is and what the other arguments are. The most recent research that include SRL in the SMT pipeline was done for MT evaluation. The MEANT family of metrics are semantic evaluation metrics that correlate more closely with human adequacy judgements than the commonly used surface based metrics (Lo and Wu, 2011, 2012; Lo *et al.*, 2012; Lo and Wu, 2013b; Macháček and Bojar, 2013).

Unlike *n*-gram or edit-distance based metrics, the MEANT family of metrics (Lo and Wu, 2011, 2012; Lo *et al.*, 2012) adopt the principle that a good translation is one in which humans can successfully understand the general meaning of the input sentence as captured by the basic event structure defined in (Pradhan *et al.*, 2004). Recent works have shown that the semantic frame based metric, MEANT, correlates better with human adequacy judgment than common evaluation metrics (Lo and Wu, 2011, 2012;

Algorithm Token based ITG-indcution and alignment.

$$
\begin{aligned}
&C && \triangleright \text{The parallel corpus}\\
&c && \triangleright \text{The rule counts}\\
&G = \langle N, W_0, W_1, R, S\rangle && \triangleright \text{The empty ITG}\\
&A \in N && \triangleright \text{The bracketing symbol}\\
&p && \triangleright \text{The rule probability function to estimate}\\
&a && \triangleright \text{The alignments}\\
&sum \leftarrow 0 && \triangleright \text{The sum of all counts}\\
&R \leftarrow R \cup \{S \to A, A \to [AA], A \to \langle AA\rangle\}\\
&p(S \to A) = 1\\
&p(A \to [AA]) = \tfrac{1}{4}\\
&p(A \to \langle AA\rangle) = \tfrac{1}{4}\\
&\textbf{for } \text{parallel sentences } e_{0..T}/f_{0..V} \in C \textbf{ do}\\
&\quad \textbf{for } 0 \le s < T \textbf{ do}\\
&\qquad W_0 \leftarrow W_0 \cup \{e_{s..s+1}\}\\
&\qquad R \leftarrow R \cup \{A \to e_{s..s+1}/\epsilon\}\\
&\qquad c_{A \to e_{s..s+1}/\epsilon} \leftarrow c_{A \to e_{s..s+1}/\epsilon} + 1\\
&\qquad sum \leftarrow sum + 1\\
&\quad \textbf{for } 0 \le u < V \textbf{ do}\\
&\qquad W_1 \leftarrow W_1 \cup \{f_{u..u+1}\}\\
&\qquad R \leftarrow R \cup \{A \to \epsilon/f_{u..u+1}\}\\
&\qquad c_{A \to \epsilon/f_{u..u+1}} \leftarrow c_{A \to \epsilon/f_{u..u+1}} + 1\\
&\qquad sum \leftarrow sum + 1\\
&\quad \textbf{for } 0 \le s < T \textbf{ do}\\
&\qquad \textbf{for } 0 \le u < V \textbf{ do}\\
&\qquad\quad R \leftarrow R \cup \{A \to e_{s..s+1}/f_{u..u+1}\}\\
&\qquad\quad c_{A \to e_{s..s+1}/f_{u..u+1}} \leftarrow c_{A \to e_{s..s+1}/f_{u..u+1}} + 1\\
&\qquad\quad sum \leftarrow sum + 1\\
&\textbf{for } \text{rule } A \to e/f \in R \textbf{ do}\\
&\quad p(A \to e/f) \leftarrow \tfrac{1}{2}\tfrac{c_{A \to e/f}}{sum}\\
&\textbf{repeat}\\
&\quad p \leftarrow reestimate\_with\_em(G, p, C)\\
&\textbf{until } \text{convergence}\\
&\textbf{for } \text{parallel sentences } e_{0..T}/f_{0..V} \in C \textbf{ do}\\
&\quad a_{e_{0..T}/f_{0..V}} \leftarrow viterbi\_parse(G, p, e_{0..T}/f_{0..V})\\
&\textbf{return } a
\end{aligned}
$$

Figure 1: Token based BITG induction algorithm.

Table 2: Tuning the error penalty on the Chinese-English translation set.

Weight	cased/uncased					
	BLEU	METEOR	TER	WER	PER	CDER
0	16.29/16.63	36.9/38.9	69.09/68.69	71.34/71.03	60.78/60.22	67.89/67.44
0.01	15.93/16.34	36.4/38.6	69.14/68.77	71.80/71.42	60.99/60.43	68.29/67.87
0.1	15.77/15.99	37.0/38.9	69.30/68.90	71.85/71.48	60.46/59.90	68.18/67.76
0.5	16.90/17.19	37.9/40.1	68.85/68.53	71.53/71.26	60.14/59.61	67.44/67.18
0.6	**17.06/17.38**	**38.0/40.1**	**68.69/68.32**	**71.48/71.16**	**59.87/59.34**	**67.47/67.12**
0.9	16.34/16.60	37.4/39.3	69.80/69.33	72.33/71.96	60.75/60.19	68.58/68.18

Lo *et al.*, 2012) such as BLEU (Papineni *et al.*, 2002), NIST (Doddington, 2002), METEOR (Banerjee and Lavie, 2005), CDER (Leusch *et al.*, 2006), WER (Nießen *et al.*, 2000), and TER (Snover *et al.*, 2006). It has been shown that including semantic role labeling in the training pipeline by tuning against a semantic frame objective function such as the semantic evaluation metric MEANT (Lo *et al.*, 2013a; Lo and Wu, 2013a; Lo *et al.*, 2013b; Beloucif *et al.*, 2014) significantly improves the quality of the MT output. Beloucif *et al.* (2015) showed that injecting a crosslingual objective function into the training pipeline helps to improve the quality of the word alignment. We argue in this paper that incorporating monolingual semantic information while training SMT systems can help to learn more semantically correct bilingual correlations for low resource languages.

Table 3: Tuning the error penalty on the Hausa-English translation set.

Weight	BLEU	METEOR	TER	WER	PER	CDER
			cased/uncased			
0	16.60/17.14	44.8/47.8	70.63/69.69	73.16/72.46	58.24/56.77	69.59/68.71
0.01	16.83/17.37	43.9/46.7	71.06/70.08	73.62/72.85	58.96/57.36	70.05/69.02
0.1	17.35/17.87	44.6/47.6	69.99/69.05	72.65/71.93	58.17/56.59	69.10/68.08
0.5	17.10/17.57	44.2/47.2	70.39/69.50	72.92/72.19	58.92/57.47	69.45/68.49
0.6	**17.44/17.98**	**45.0/47.9**	**69.94/68.92**	**72.47/71.77**	**58.18/56.70**	**68.92/67.97**
0.9	16.99/17.49	44.9/48.0	70.18/69.21	72.78/56.55	58.08/56.55	69.17/68.24

3 Semantic frame based ITG induction for low resource languages

3.1 Word alignment

We implement a token based BITG system as our ITG baseline. Our choice of BITG constraints is based on previous work that has shown that BITG based alignments outperformed GIZA++ alignments (Saers *et al.*, 2009).

Figure 1 shows the BITG induction algorithm that we use in this paper. We initialize it with uniform structural probabilities, setting aside half of the probability mass for lexical rules. This probability mass is distributed among the lexical rules according to co-occurrence counts from the training data, assuming each sentence contains one empty token to account for singletons. These initial probabilities are refined with 10 iterations of expectation maximization where the expectation step is calculated using beam pruned parsing (Saers *et al.*, 2009) with a beam width of 100. In the last iteration, we extract the alignments imposed by the Viterbi parses as the word alignments outputted by the system.

Our proposed model injects a monolingual semantic frame based objective function into the BITG induction phase. We introduce an error weight between 0 and 1, that the inside probability is multiplied by if the English side of a bispan crosses any of the spans in the English SRL parse. The details of the approach are as follows:

$$\alpha' = \begin{cases} \alpha_{A_{s,t,u,v}} \times c_0 & \text{if } \forall_{(i,j)} \quad \begin{aligned} &i \leq s \wedge j \leq s, \\ &s \leq i \wedge j \leq t, \\ &t \leq i \wedge t \leq j, \\ &i \leq s \wedge t \leq j, \end{aligned} \\ \alpha & \text{otherwise} \end{cases} \tag{2}$$

where α represents the inside probabliity, α' is the new estimated inside probability, (s,t) are the output language sentence spans, (i,j) are the English SRL parse spans. To ensure that we are not testing on any training data, we are doing something unusual: we tune the error weights on two different languages, and then test the best error weight on a third language. To test our method on Uzbek-English translations, we first tune the error weights using two language pairs: Chinese-English and Hausa-English translation. For both language pairs, we tune the error weights via grid search. Tables 2 and 3 represent the results that we got by experimenting with different error weights in both Chinese-English and Hausa-English test sets respectively. The best error weight that we got from both tunings equals to 0.6. We then apply the optimized selected weight to train an Uzbek-English translation model. This error weight is multiplied by the inside probabilities α during the BITG training if the English side of the ITG bispan crosses the English SRL parse as described in the function above.

We also train 10 iterations of EM of the new model and use Viterbi parsing to extract the alignments. We contrast the performance of our proposed monolingual semantic frame based alignment to the conventional BITG alignment and to the traditional GIZA++ baseline with grow-diag-final-and to harmonize both alignment directions.

Table 4: Translation quality of an Uzbek-English phrase based SMT system build on three different alignment methods.

Alignments	cased/uncased					
	BLEU	METEOR	TER	WER	PER	CDER
GIZA++	16.28/17.09	40.7/42.8	82.20/80.91	88.51/87.71	66.70/64.61	79.47/78.11
BITG	16.85/17.66	38.8/40.9	79.75/78.12	85.53/84.60	65.04/62.89	76.93/75.51
Monolingual English SRL	**17.40/18.15**	**41.0/43.4**	**79.25/77.72**	**85.20/84.48**	**63.29/61.13**	**76.36/75.00**

Input
Mamlakatimizga tashrif buyurgan Indoneziya Respublikasi tashqi ishlar vaziri Hasan Virayuda 13 may kuni O'zbekiston Respublikasi Oliy Majlisi Qonunchilik palatasi Spikeri Dilorom Toshmuhamedova bilan uchr ashdi

Ref
Foreign Minister of Indonesia Hasan Wirayuda met Speaker of the Legislative Chamber of Oliy Majlis of Uzbekistan Dilorom Tashmuhamedova on 13 May .

Giza++
is on a visit in Uzbekistan Minister of Foreign Affairs of the Republic of Indonesia Hasan Wirayuda said on 13 May , he met the Speaker of the Legislative Chamber of Oliy Majlis of Uzbekistan Dilorom Tashmuhamedova

BITG
Members of the delegation , headed by the Minister of Foreign Affairs of the Republic of Indonesia Hasan Wirayuda on May 13 , she met the Speaker of the Legislative Chamber of Oliy Majlis of Uzbekistan Dilorom Tashmuhamedova .

Proposed model
the Minister of Foreign Affairs of the Republic of Indonesia Hasan Wirayuda on 13 May , he met the Speaker of the Legislative Chamber of Oliy Majlis of Uzbekistan Dilorom Tashmuhamedova.

Figure 2: An example extracted from the test data for the Uzbek-English translations.

3.2   Baseline

Our experiments are part of the DARPA LORELEI study on efficient learning under low resource conditions therefore we purposely use relatively small corpora in different languages. We tried to show that including semantic frames earlier in learning SMT systems can help us to learn from relatively small corpora, in contrast to traditional SMT training models, which require expensive huge corpora. Table 1 represents the size of the three datasets used for our experimental setup. We tried to vary the data size and the language family for tuning the error weight and testing our proposed model to show that our approach is not language dependent and can easily be generalized across languages. We adopted the DARPA LORELEI program approach by using a relatively small Chinese corpus, a medium Hausa corpus and a slightly larger Uzbek corpus, we show that our approach is able to learn from small to medium datasets and does not rely on heavy memorization.

We tested the different alignments described above by using the standard MOSES toolkit (Koehn *et al.*, 2007), and a 4-gram language model learned with the SRI language model toolkit (Stolcke, 2002) trained on the training data of each language respectively. To tune the loglinear mixture weights, we use k-best MIRA (Cherry and Foster, 2012), a version of margin-based classification algorithm or MIRA (Chiang, 2012).

4 Results

We compared the performance of the semantic frame based BITG alignments against both the conventional token based BITG alignments and the traditional GIZA++ alignments. We evaluated our MT output using the surface based evaluation metrics BLEU (Papineni *et al.*, 2002), METEOR (Banerjee and Lavie, 2005), CDER (Leusch *et al.*, 2006), WER (Nießen *et al.*, 2000), and TER (Snover *et al.*, 2006). Table 4 represents the result of testing our approach with the best tuned weight on Uzbek-English translations. We see that the alignment based on our proposed algorithm helps to achieve much higher scores across all metrics in comparison to both conventional BITG and GIZA++ alignments.

Figure 2 shows an interesting example extracted from the Uzbek-English translations, and compares the performance of our proposed model to both a GIZA++ based model and a BITG based model. We notice that our proposed model gives the output that best reflects the meaning of the sentence according to the reference translation. GIZA++ gives a relatively bad translation. BITG based model mixes the gender of "the prime minister Hasan Wirayuda" and refers to him by "she" instead of "he". Our proposed model on the other hand, is able to capture the general meaning of the sentence, and produces a relatively fluent output in comparison to both GIZA++ and BITG.

The results and examples we see above show that we should be more focused on incorporating semantic information during the actual early stage learning of the structure of the translation model, rather than merely tuning a handful of late stage loglinear mixture weights against a semantic objective function.

5 Conclusion

In this paper we have presented a semantically driven alignment method for low resource languages, where we use an English monolingual semantic frame parse and translation lexicons for BITG induction. We have shown that including a semantic frame based objective function at an early stage of learning SMT training helps to improve the quality of the MT translation for low resource languages. We experimented on three different language pairs from the DARPA LORELEI study on efficient learning under low resource conditions and have demonstrated that using a semantic frame based objective function during the actual learning of the translation model helps to learn good bilingual correlations with a relatively small dataset in contrast to conventional SMT systems.

Finally, we have shown that our proposed system produces a more semantically correct alignment and thus yields an improvement in comparison to the conventional BITG alignments and to the traditional GIZA++ alignments.

References

Karteek Addanki, Chi-kiu Lo, Markus Saers, and Dekai Wu. LTG vs. ITG coverage of cross-lingual verb frame alternations. In *16th Annual Conference of the European Association for Machine Translation (EAMT-2012)*, Trento, Italy, May 2012.

Alfred V. Aho and Jeffrey D. Ullman. *The Theory of Parsing, Translation, and Compiling*. Prentice-Halll, Englewood Cliffs, New Jersey, 1972.

Satanjeev Banerjee and Alon Lavie. METEOR: An automatic metric for MT evaluation with improved correlation with human judgments. In *Workshop on Intrinsic and Extrinsic Evaluation Measures for Machine Translation and/or Summarization*, Ann Arbor, Michigan, June 2005.

Meriem Beloucif, Chi kiu Lo, and Dekai Wu. Improving meant based semantically tuned smt. In *11 th International Workshop on spoken Language Translation (IWSLT 2014), 34-41 Lake Tahoe, California*, 2014.

Meriem Beloucif, Markus Saers, and Dekai Wu. Improving semantic smt via soft semantic role label constraints on itg alignments. In *Machine Translation Summit XV (MT Summit 2015)*, pages 333–345, Miami, USA, October 2015.

Phil Blunsom, Trevor Cohn, Chris Dyer, and Miles Osborne. A Gibbs sampler for phrasal synchronous grammar induction. In *Joint Conference of the 47th Annual Meeting of the Association for Computational Linguistics and 4th International Joint Conference on Natural Language Processing of the AFNLP (ACL-IJCNLP 2009)*, pages 782–790, Suntec, Singapore, August 2009.

Peter F. Brown, John Cocke, Stephen A. Della Pietra, Vincent J. Della Pietra, Frederik Jelinek, John D. Lafferty, Robert L. Mercer, and Paul S. Roossin. A statistical approach to machine translation. *Computational Linguistics*, 16(2):79–85, 1990.

Peter F. Brown, Stephen A. Della Pietra, Vincent J. Della Pietra, and Robert L. Mercer. The mathematics of machine translation: Parameter estimation. *Computational Linguistics*, 19(2):263–311, 1993.

Colin Cherry and George Foster. Batch tuning strategies for statistical machine translation. In *Proceedings of the 2012 Conference of the North American Chapter of the ACL: Human Language Technologies*. Association for Computational Linguistics, 2012.

Colin Cherry and Dekang Lin. Inversion transduction grammar for joint phrasal translation modeling. In *Syntax and Structure in Statistical Translation (SSST)*, pages 17–24, Rochester, New York, April 2007.

David Chiang. Hierarchical phrase-based translation. *Computational Linguistics*, 33(2):201–228, 2007.

David Chiang. Hope and fear for discriminative training of statistical translation models. *The Journal of Machine Learning Research*, 13:1159–1187, April 2012.

Adrià De Gispert, Deepa Gupta, Maja Popovic, Patrik Lambert, Jose B.Marino, Marcello Federico, Hermann Ney, and Rafael Banchs. Improving statistical word alignment with morpho-syntactic transformations. In *Advances in Natural Language Processing*, pages 368–379, 2006.

George Doddington. Automatic evaluation of machine translation quality using n-gram co-occurrence statistics. In *The second international conference on Human Language Technology Research (HLT '02)*, San Diego, California, 2002.

Chris Dyer, Jonathan Clark, Alon Lavie, and Noah A.Smith. Unsupervised word alignment with arbitrary features. In *49th Annual Meeting of the Association for Computational Linguistics*, 2011.

Daniel Gildea and Daniel Jurafsky. Automatic labeling of semantic roles. *Computational Linguistics*, 28(3):245–288, 2002.

Aria Haghighi, John Blitzer, John DeNero, and Dan Klein. Better word alignments with supervised ITG models. In *Joint Conference of the 47th Annual Meeting of the Association for Computational Linguistics and 4th International Joint Conference on Natural Language Processing of the AFNLP (ACL-IJCNLP 2009)*, pages 923–931, Suntec, Singapore, August 2009.

Philipp Koehn, Hieu Hoang, Alexandra Birch, Chris Callison-Burch, Marcello Federico, Nicola Bertoldi, Brooke Cowan, Wade Shen, Christine Moran, Richard Zens, Chris Dyer, Ondrej Bojar, Alexandra Constantin, and Evan Herbst. Moses: Open source toolkit for statistical machine translation. In *Interactive Poster and Demonstration Sessions of the 45th Annual Meeting of the Association for Computational Linguistics (ACL 2007)*, pages 177–180, Prague, Czech Republic, June 2007.

Gregor Leusch, Nicola Ueffing, and Hermann Ney. CDer: Efficient MT evaluation using block movements. In *11th Conference of the European Chapter of the Association for Computational Linguistics (EACL-2006)*, 2006.

Philip M. Lewis and Richard E. Stearns. Syntax-directed transduction. *Journal of the Association for Computing Machinery*, 15(3):465–488, 1968.

Chi-kiu Lo and Dekai Wu. MEANT: An inexpensive, high-accuracy, semi-automatic metric for evaluating translation utility based on semantic roles. In *49th Annual Meeting of the Association for Computational Linguistics: Human Language Technologies (ACL HLT 2011)*, 2011.

Chi-kiu Lo and Dekai Wu. Unsupervised vs. supervised weight estimation for semantic MT evaluation metrics. In *Sixth Workshop on Syntax, Semantics and Structure in Statistical Translation (SSST-6)*, 2012.

Chi-kiu Lo and Dekai Wu. Can informal genres be better translated by tuning on automatic semantic metrics? In *14th Machine Translation Summit (MT Summit XIV)*, 2013.

Chi-kiu Lo and Dekai Wu. MEANT at WMT 2013: A tunable, accurate yet inexpensive semantic frame based mt evaluation metric. In *8th Workshop on Statistical Machine Translation (WMT 2013)*, 2013.

Chi-kiu Lo, Anand Karthik Tumuluru, and Dekai Wu. Fully automatic semantic MT evaluation. In *7th Workshop on Statistical Machine Translation (WMT 2012)*, 2012.

Chi-kiu Lo, Karteek Addanki, Markus Saers, and Dekai Wu. Improving machine translation by training against an automatic semantic frame based evaluation metric. In *51st Annual Meeting of the Association for Computational Linguistics (ACL 2013)*, 2013.

Chi-kiu Lo, Meriem Beloucif, and Dekai Wu. Improving machine translation into Chinese by tuning against Chinese MEANT. In *International Workshop on Spoken Language Translation (IWSLT 2013)*, 2013.

Jeff Ma, Spyros Matsoukas, and Richard Schwartz. Improving low-resource statistical machine translation with a novel semantic word clustering algorithm. In *Proceedings of the MT Summit XIII*, 2011.

Matouš Macháček and Ondřej Bojar. Results of the WMT13 metrics shared task. In *Eighth Workshop on Statistical Machine Translation (WMT 2013)*, Sofia, Bulgaria, August 2013.

Graham Neubig, Taro Watanabe, Eiichiro Sumita, Shinsuke Mori, and Tatsuya Kawahara. An unsupervised model for joint phrase alignment and extraction. In *49th Annual Meeting of the Association for Computational Linguistics: Human Language Technologies (ACL HLT 2011)*, pages 632–641, Portland, Oregon, June 2011.

Sonja Nießen, Franz Josef Och, Gregor Leusch, and Hermann Ney. A evaluation tool for machine translation: Fast evaluation for MT research. In *The Second International Conference on Language Resources and Evaluation (LREC 2000)*, 2000.

Franz Josef Och and Hermann Ney. Improved statistical alignment models. In *The 38th Annual Meeting of the Association for Computational Linguistics (ACL 2000)*, pages 440–447, Hong Kong, October 2000.

Martha Palmer, Daniel Gildea, and Paul Kingsbury. The proposition bank: an annotated corpus of semantic roles. *Computational Linguistics*, 31(1):71–106, 2005.

Kishore Papineni, Salim Roukos, Todd Ward, and Wei-Jing Zhu. BLEU: a method for automatic evaluation of machine translation. In *40th Annual Meeting of the Association for Computational Linguistics (ACL-02)*, pages 311–318, Philadelphia, Pennsylvania, July 2002.

Sameer Pradhan, Wayne Ward, Kadri Hacioglu, James H. Martin, and Dan Jurafsky. Shallow semantic parsing using support vector machines. In *Human Language Technology Conference of the North American Chapter of the Association for Computational Linguistics (HLT-NAACL 2004)*, 2004.

Markus Saers and Dekai Wu. Improving phrase-based translation via word alignments from stochastic inversion transduction grammars. In *Third Workshop on Syntax and Structure in Statistical Translation (SSST-3)*, pages 28–36, Boulder, Colorado, June 2009.

Markus Saers, Joakim Nivre, and Dekai Wu. Learning stochastic bracketing inversion transduction grammars with a cubic time biparsing algorithm. In *11th International Conference on Parsing Technologies (IWPT'09)*, pages 29–32, Paris, France, October 2009.

Markus Saers, Joakim Nivre, and Dekai Wu. Word alignment with stochastic bracketing linear inversion transduction grammar. In *Human Language Technologies: The 2010 Annual Conference of the North American Chapter of the Association for Computational Linguistics (NAACL HLT 2010)*, pages 341–344, Los Angeles, California, June 2010.

Matthew Snover, Bonnie Dorr, Richard Schwartz, Linnea Micciulla, and John Makhoul. A study of translation edit rate with targeted human annotation. In *7th Biennial Conference Association for Machine Translation in the Americas (AMTA 2006)*, pages 223–231, Cambridge, Massachusetts, August 2006.

Theerawat Songyot and David Chiang. Improving word alignment using word similarity. In *52nd Annual Meeting of the Association for Computational Linguistics*, 2014.

Andreas Stolcke. SRILM – an extensible language modeling toolkit. In *7th International Conference on Spoken Language Processing (ICSLP 2002 - INTERSPEECH 2002)*, pages 901–904, Denver, Colorado, September 2002.

Stephan Vogel, Hermann Ney, and Christoph Tillmann. HMM-based word alignment in statistical translation. In *The 16th International Conference on Computational linguistics (COLING-96)*, volume 2, pages 836–841, 1996.

Dekai Wu. Trainable coarse bilingual grammars for parallel text bracketing. In *Third Annual Workshop on Very Large Corpora (WVLC-3)*, pages 69–81, Cambridge, Massachusetts, June 1995.

Dekai Wu. Stochastic inversion transduction grammars and bilingual parsing of parallel corpora. *Computational Linguistics*, 23(3):377–403, 1997.

Richard Zens and Hermann Ney. A comparative study on reordering constraints in statistical machine translation. In *41st Annual Meeting of the Association for Computational Linguistics (ACL-2003)*, pages 144–151, Stroudsburg, Pennsylvania, 2003.

Hao Zhang and Daniel Gildea. Stochastic lexicalized inversion transduction grammar for alignment. In *43rd Annual Meeting of the Association for Computational Linguistics (ACL-05)*, pages 475–482, Ann Arbor, Michigan, June 2005.

Using Bilingual Segments in Generating Word-to-word Translations

K. M. Kavitha[1,3]   **Luís Gomes**[1,2]   **José Gabriel Pereira Lopes**[1,2]

[1]NOVA Laboratory for Computer Science and Informatics (NOVA LINCS)
Faculdade de Ciências e Tecnologia, Universidade Nova de Lisboa
2829-516 Caparica, Portugal.
`luismsgomes@gmail.com  gpl@fct.unl.pt`
[2]ISTRION BOX-Translation & Revision, Lda., Parkurbis, Covilhã 6200-865 Portugal.
[3] Department of Computer Applications, St Joseph Engineering College
Vamanjoor, Mangaluru, 575 028, India.
`kavitham@sjec.ac.in`

Abstract

We defend that bilingual lexicons automatically extracted from parallel corpora, whose entries have been meanwhile validated by linguists and classified as correct or incorrect, should constitute a specific parallel corpora. And, in this paper, we propose to use word-to-word translations to learn morph-units (comprising of bilingual stems and suffixes) from those bilingual lexicons for two language pairs L1-L2 and L1-L3 to induce a bilingual lexicon for the language pair L2-L3, apart from also learning morph-units for this other language pair. The applicability of bilingual morph-units in L1-L2 and L1-L3 is examined from the perspective of pivot-based lexicon induction for language pair L2-L3 with L1 as bridge. While the lexicon is derived by transitivity, the correspondences are identified based on previously learnt bilingual stems and suffixes rather than surface translation forms. The induced pairs are validated using a binary classifier trained on morphological and similarity-based features using an existing, automatically acquired, manually validated bilingual translation lexicon for language pair L2-L3. In this paper, we discuss the use of English (EN)-French (FR) and English (EN)-Portuguese (PT) lexicon of word-to-word translations in generating word-to-word translations for the language pair FR-PT with EN as pivot language. Generated translations are filtered out first using an SVM-based FR-PT classifier and then are manually validated.

1   Introduction

Translation lexicon coverage is one of the crucial factors influencing effective Machine Translation. To fill in the gap corresponding to certain missing translation pairs and/or to overcome the difficulties in acquiring translation lexicons for under-resourced language pairs, one can combine the already available bilingual knowledge bases using a common language referred to as pivot and hence automatically expand the translation coverage. Although the pivoted approach to lexicon induction is not new, the novelty of our approach lies in the use of bilingual morph-units rather than the surface translation forms.

We depart from 3 bilingual lexicons (EN-PT, EN-FR and FR-PT) that were automatically acquired from aligned parallel corpora using various extraction techniques (Brown et al., 1993; Lardilleux and Lepage, 2009; Aires et al., 2009; Gomes and Lopes, 2011), whose entries were classified as correct or incorrect by linguists making use of a bilingual concordancer (Costa et al., 2015). These lexicons will hence and along the paper be named as *validated bilingual lexicons*. To be specific, we discuss the use of EN-FR and EN-PT validated bilingual lexicons in inducing bilingual pairs for FR-PT with EN as the pivot language.

The task of bilingual lexicon augmentation is approached in two phases involving pivoted induction and binary classification for subsequent validation of the induced pairs, followed by manual validation. One of the concerns with pivoted translation induction is the generation of wrong translations primarily due to polysemy and ambiguous words. Hence, prior to human validation, for selecting the induced translations in FR-PT, an automatic filter in the form of an SVM-based binary classifier trained on the validated FR-PT bilingual lexicon is used. For every pair of newly induced morph-units/words in the first phase, the next phase involves determining whether the two are translations of each other or not.

Proceedings of the Sixth Workshop on Hybrid Approaches to Translation,
pages 61–71, Osaka, Japan, December 11, 2016.

2 Related Work

While the idea of using pivot language(s) for deriving bilingual lexicon is not new, the approaches differ with respect to the resources employed (Ács, 2014) (Wushouer et al., 2014b), languages dealt (Saralegi et al., 2012) (Wushouer et al., 2013) and the post-processing operations involved in selecting unambiguous and correct translations (Tanaka and Umemura, 1994) (Kaji and Erdenebat, 2008) (Shezaf and Rappoport, 2010). Earliest reported work on pivoted dictionary induction is credited to Tanaka et al. (Tanaka and Umemura, 1994), who proposed the Inverse consultation (IC) approach for pruning wrong translation candidates. Paik et al. (Paik et al., 2004) argued on the importance of directionality in automating the dictionary building process. His experiments are based on one-time inverse consultation method earlier proposed by Tanaka et al. (Tanaka and Umemura, 1994), the overlapping constraint method for improved equivalent pair extraction rate and the POS-based sorting of newly linked pairs to avoid polysemous entries.

In an exclusive analysis of the techniques used to filter wrong translation candidates induced by pivoting, Saralegi et al. (Saralegi et al., 2011) explored two of the common choices, namely the Inverse consultation (IC) method (Tanaka and Umemura, 1994) and the Distributional Similarity measure (DS) (Kaji and Erdenebat, 2008). An outcome of their analysis is that, IC relies on large number of lexical variants in the dictionaries for each sense in the pivot language. Further, given that DS identifies as translations those words exhibiting similar distributions or contexts across two corpora of different languages, it is learnt that, richer context representations and the translation quality of contexts contribute to its improved performance. Union and linear combination of IC and DS outperforms each of these measures taken individually. The authors (Saralegi et al., 2012) thereon discuss the applicability of these methods in building a Basque-Chinese dictionary via English. In a heuristic based approach, Wushouer et al. (Wushouer et al., 2013) explores the use of probability, semantics and spelling similarity heuristics for inducing one-to-one mapping dictionary of Uyghur and Kazakh languages from Chinese-Uyghur and Chinese-Kazakh dictionaries.

In a different study, transitive lexicon induction is centred on multilingual lexical databases such as, lexicon of language-specific word variants, lexemes and collocations, with the validation of new pairs achieved through parallel corpus consultation (Nerima and Wehrli, 2008). Another research (Ács, 2014) on augmenting existing dictionaries in multiple languages, relies on Wiktionary for exploring the links between translations. While exploiting the fact that pairs found via several pivot languages are more precise than those found via one (Tanaka and Umemura, 1994), Ács (Ács, 2014) proposes to extend IC (Tanaka and Umemura, 1994) from using single pivot up to 53 pivots (Ács, 2014). Addressing the task as an optimisation problem, Wushouer et al. (Wushouer et al., 2014a; Wushouer et al., 2014b), proposed extended constraint optimisation model, formalised on Integer Linear Programming for pivot-based dictionary induction of closely related languages by employing multiple dictionaries.

In each of the afore-mentioned approaches, new correspondences are induced by exploiting surface translation forms in two language pairs with one or more language(s) as bridge. In contrast, our approach deviates from transitive induction scheme discussed above with respect to the resources employed in learning correspondences. A specific distinction in our approach is that the resources used for pivoting consist of bilingual morph-units learnt using the bilingual learning method (Karimbi Mahesh et al., 2014a), unlike the traditional surface translation forms. To be specific, for each language pair the knowledge base employed in the experiments consists of bilingual stems, bilingual suffixes as explained in Section 3 and illustrated in Table 1.

3 Background - Bilingual Segments as Knowledge Base

Fundamental to the pivoted induction strategy are the bilingual resources comprising of *bilingual stems* and *bilingual suffixes* learnt from validated bilingual lexicons for the language pairs EN-FR and EN-PT extracted from the aligned parallel corpora[1] using various extraction techniques (Brown et al., 1993; Lardilleux and Lepage, 2009; Gomes, 2009; Aires et al., 2009; Gomes and Lopes, 2011). The methods proposed by Brown et al. (Brown et al., 1993) and Lardilleux and Lepage (Lardilleux and Lepage,

---

[1]DGT-TM - https://open-data.europa.eu/en/data/dataset/dgt-translation-memory
Europarl - http://www.statmt.org/europarl/
OPUS (EUconst, EMEA) - http://opus.lingfil.uu.se/

2009) were employed for an initial extraction as they do not require a priori validated lexicons. The former is based on corpus-wide frequency counts and provides an alignment for every word in the corpus, while the latter is based on random sub-corpus sampling, improving precision for some words but being omissive with respect to others. The alignment method proposed by Gomes (Gomes, 2009) projects the validated bilingual lexicons into the parallel corpus, aligning known expressions, and leaving the remainder words unaligned. The extraction method proposed by Aires et al. (Aires et al., 2009) uses these alignments as anchors to infer alignments of neighbouring unaligned words, based on co-occurrence statistics. Finally, the method proposed by Gomes and Lopes (Gomes and Lopes, 2011) combines these co-occurrence statistics with a spelling similarity score, SpSim, which is trained to recognize cognate words by learning regular spelling differences from previously validated bilingual cognates such as [ph]arm[a]c[y]↔[f]arm[á]c[ia] (EN-PT).

Induction of bilingual stems and suffixes follows the bilingual learning approach (Karimbi Mahesh et al., 2014a) applied on the bilingual lexicon of word-to-word translations for each of the language pairs EN-PT and EN-FR. The approach being purely suffixation based induces bilingual stems, suffixes and bilingual suffix replacement rules that allow one translation form to be obtained from the other (by identifying clusters of bilingual suffixes that associate with a set of induced bilingual stems). The bilingual stems and suffixes learnt, when productively combined, enable new translations to be suggested. Collectively, these bilingual stems and suffixes are referred to as *bilingual morph-units* and are fundamental to the pivoted translation suggestion task elaborated in the forthcoming sections. A bilingual stem conflates various inflected surface forms of a translation. The bilingual suffixes represent morphological extensions for the bilingual stems. The approach is illustrated below for the language pair EN-FR.

1. Decompose each bilingual pair in the lexicon as bilingual stems and bilingual suffixes by pairing similar translations.
   Example: Split pair of translations 'ensured' ⇔ 'assuré' and 'ensuring' ⇔ 'assurer' into bilingual stem ('ensur' ⇔ 'assur') with bilingual morphological extensions ('ed', 'é') and ('ing', 'er').

2. Group all the bilingual suffixes that associate with each of the bilingual stem identified in Step 1. Hence identify the bilingual suffix transformations (replacement rules). Each such grouping indicates the possibility of obtaining one surface form from another.
   Example:
   ('ensure', 'assure') : ('', 'r') ('d', 'ée') ('d', 'és') ('d', 'ées') ('d', 'é')
   ('ensur', 'assur') : ('e', 'er') ('ed', 'é') ('ed', 'ée') ('ing', 'er') ('ed', 'és') ('ed', 'ées')
   represent randomly selected groupings learnt from inflected translation forms 'ensured' ⇔ 'assuré', 'ensuring' ⇔ 'assurer' and so forth.

3. Eliminate redundant groups by retaining those bilingual stems that share higher number of transformations.
   Example: Among the two examples in the step 2, the second group ('ensur', 'assur') : ('e', 'er') ('ed', 'é') ('ed', 'ée') ('ing', 'er') ('ed', 'és') ('ed', 'ées') is retained.

4. Generalise the bilingual suffix replacement rules by looking for other bilingual stems sharing identical transformations. In other words, this involves identification of bilingual suffix clusters (set of bilingual stems sharing same bilingual suffix transformations).
   Example: ('increas', 'augment'): ('e', 'er') ('ed', 'é') ('ed', 'ée') ('ing', 'er') ('ed', 'és') ('ed', 'ées') represents another grouping, where the bilingual stem ('increas', 'augment') shares same bilingual morphological extensions as the bilingual stem ('ensur', 'assur') and hence both bilingual stems belong to the same cluster.

The partition approach provided in the clustering tool kit CLUTO[2] was used to identify the clusters of bilingual suffixes.

4   Approach Outline

The proposed approach works in two phases. Given the list of bilingual stems learnt from validated bilingual lexicons for the language pairs EN-FR and EN-PT as briefed in the Section 3, we derive a lexicon

____
[2]http://glaros.dtc.umn.edu/gkhome/views/cluto

of bilingual stems for the language pair FR-PT by inducing transitive correspondences between bilingual stems of EN-FR and EN-PT with the common language EN. Having determined the bilingual stems for the language pair FR-PT as mentioned, the associated morphological extensions in the form of bilingual suffixes are gathered for each newly induced bilingual stem based on the transitive correspondences between bilingual suffixes for EN-FR and EN-PT. We impose the constraint that, the bilingual suffixes representing transitive correspondences should occur substantial number of times in the reference set of bilingual suffixes learnt from FR-PT validated lexicon. Newly induced correspondences require validation, as not all of the generated translations are correct. Thus post-generation, prior to manual validation, we classify the generated pairs into one of the pre-defined correct or incorrect classes.

Table 1: Known stem, suffix correspondences for EN-PT and EN-FR (rows 1, 2) and the associated transitive correspondences learnt for FR-PT (row 3)

Language Pair	Bilingual Stems		Bilingual Suffixes
EN-FR	('deliver', 'délivr')	('', 'er')	('ed', 'é'), ('ed', 'és')
EN-PT	('deliver', 'emit')	('', 'ir')	('ed', 'ido'), ('ed', 'iu')
FR-PT	('délivr', 'emit')	('er', 'ir')	('é', 'ido'), ('é', 'iu'), ('és', 'ido'), ('és', 'iu')

Table 1 instantiates the use of EN-FR and EN-PT bilingual morph-units in learning new correspondences for FR-PT, with EN as the pivot language. In the second column of the table, the second and the third rows respectively show the known bilingual stems for each of the language pairs EN-FR and EN-PT. Similarly, the following columns in the second and third rows show the known bilingual suffixes attached to the corresponding bilingual stems shown in column 2. The last row shows the newly induced stem pairs for the target language pair FR-PT and their associated morphological extensions (suffix pairs) obtained by transitivity.

4.1 Pivoting Stem and Suffix Correspondences

First, using the list of bilingual stems for two language pairs L1-L2 and L1-L3 represented as relational tables, we perform a relational natural join over common stem in language L1[3].

Algorithm 1 Translation Generation as Pivoting and Classification

---

1: **procedure** PIVOT_BILINGUALMORPHS
2:     A_{L1-L2}, A_{L1-L3} ← lexicon of bilingual stems for L1-L2, L1-L3
3:     S_{L2-L3} ← bilingual suffix list learnt from validated lexicon for L2-L3
4:     Join relational tables for A_{L1-L2} and A_{L1-L3} on stems of the common language L1
5:     **for** each stem pair $(a_{i_{L1}}, a_{i_{L2}}) \epsilon A_{L1-L2}$ and $(a_{i_{L1}}, a_{i_{L3}}) \epsilon A_{L1-L3}$ **do**
6:         **if** suffix pair $(s_{i_{L1}}, s_{i_{L2}}) \epsilon$ bilingual suffix list associated with $(a_{i_{L1}}, a_{i_{L2}})$ &&
7:             suffix pair $(s_{i_{L1}}, s_{i_{L3}}) \epsilon$ bilingual suffix list associated with $(a_{i_{L1}}, a_{i_{L3}})$ **then**
8:             append $(s_{i_{L2}}, s_{i_{L3}})$ to the suffix list associated with $(a_{i_{L2}}, a_{i_{L3}})$ **iff**
9:             $(s_{i_{L2}}, s_{i_{L3}}) \epsilon S_{L2-L3}$ && $occurrence\_frequeny(s_{i_{L2}}, s_{i_{L3}}) \geq 3$.
10:         **end if**
11:     **end for**
12: **end procedure**

Let A_{L1-L2} and A_{L1-L3} be the lexicons consisting of bilingual stems for the language pairs L1-L2 and L1-L3 respectively. Further, let S_{L2-L3} be the list of bilingual suffixes learnt from validated lexicon for L2-L3. This list of bilingual suffixes is obtained by applying the bilingual learning approach (Karimbi Mahesh et al., 2014a) on the validated bilingual lexicon for L2-L3. The list serves in identifying valid bilingual suffixes from the set of candidate bilingual suffixes (for L2-L3) induced following

---

[3]Alternatively, we may perform search and replace operation on the bilingual stem file for L1-L3 using a two-column table (consisting of stems in L1 as first column and their corresponding translations in L2 as the second column) for L1-L2.

transitive correspondences between the bilingual suffixes for L1-L2 and L1-L3 over common suffix in L1 (L1 is the pivot language).

Initially, we perform a natural join on the relational tables for the bilingual lexicons A_{L1-L2} and A_{L1-L3} over common stems of the pivot language L1. Consequently, we obtain a lexicon of candidate bilingual stems for the language pairs L2-L3.

After the candidate bilingual stems are determined for the language pair L2-L3 as specified, the associated bilingual suffixes are predicted for each induced bilingual stem in L2-L3 based on the transitive correspondences between bilingual suffixes for L1-L2 and L1-L3 over common suffix in L1 (as enumerated in the steps 3 through 9 of the Algorithm 1). However, this results in an exhaustive list of candidate bilingual suffix correspondences, for each candidate bilingual stem induced in the previous step. Hence, the selection of valid correspondences from this initial list of candidate bilingual suffix correspondences is done in consultation with S_{L2-L3}, the list of known bilingual suffixes for L2-L3, i.e., valid correspondences between suffixes in L2 and L3 are determined based on their occurrence frequencies in S_{L2-L3}. Candidate bilingual suffixes (following transitive correspondences between suffixes in L1-L2 and L1-L3) with occurrence frequency less than 3 as observed in the bilingual suffix list for L2-L3 are discarded. Setting the occurrence frequency threshold below this value leads to over-generation of surface translation forms dropping the translation generation precision below 60%.

To illustrate the above outlined procedure, consider the examples in Table 1. The last row in the table represents the newly induced bilingual correspondences for FR-PT following the transitive correspondences between bilingual stems and suffixes in EN-FR (second row) and EN-PT (third row). For example, ('délivr', 'emit') represents the new bilingual stem induced following transitive correspondences between the known bilingual stems ('deliver', 'délivr') in EN-FR and ('deliver', 'emit') in EN-PT. The candidate bilingual suffixes that associate with ('délivr', 'emit') are ('er', 'ir') following the transitive correspondences between bilingual suffixes ('', 'er') in EN-FR and ('', 'ir') in EN-PT and similarly, ('é', 'ido'), ('é', 'iu'), ('és', 'ido') and ('és', 'iu') following correspondences between ('ed', 'é') in EN-FR and ('ed', 'ido'), ('ed', 'iu') in EN-PT and between ('ed', 'és') in EN-FR and ('ed', 'ido'), ('ed', 'iu') in EN-PT. Looking for the occurrence frequencies of each of these correspondences in the FR-PT bilingual suffix list, S_{FR-PT}, learnt from validated FR-PT lexicon, we choose to either retain or discard the associated suffixes.

4.2 Generation of Surface forms

Surface translation forms can be interpreted as the concatenation of newly induced bilingual stems and their associated suffixes. For instance, simple concatenation of the bilingual stem ('délivr', 'emit') with associated bilingual suffix ('er', 'ir') yields the surface form ('délivrer', 'emitir').

4.3 Validation as Binary Classification

We evaluate the newly induced FR-PT pairs by using the validated FR-PT bilingual lexicon for supervised learning and combining varied features derived from that lexicon. We train a SVM-based binary classifier that assigns each of the induced bilingual pairs into one of the previously defined correct or incorrect classes. Features (Karimbi Mahesh et al., 2014b) characterising correct and incorrect bilingual pairs are briefed in the Subsection 4.3.1.

4.3.1 Stem and Suffix Coverage

We view a bilingual translation to be composed of two bilingual morphological segments, the bilingual stem and bilingual suffix. The stem and suffix coverage refers to the content (stem) and inflectional (suffix) coverage exhibited by the bilingual pair under evaluation. The coverage is determined as the agreement between morphological units comprising of stem in one language and its translation in another language and between their morphological extensions, respectively. The features are binary valued, each representing the *stem coverage* (MC_{stm}) and *suffix coverage* (MC_{sfx}), thus characterising the bilingual pair to be validated. For any bilingual pair, a feature value '0' indicates coverage, while '1' indicates mis-coverage, with respect to the morph-unit under evaluation (stem or suffix). The two features may be collectively referred to as the *morphological coverage* feature ($MC_{stm+sfx}$).

To check for parallelism with respect to stems, the left hand side term of the stem pair (FR-PT) to be validated is matched against the set of all stems in first language (FR), learnt from the validated lexicon (training dataset of correct translations) for FR-PT. Similarly, we check if a match is found for the right hand side of the candidate stem pair in the set of known stems for PT. If matched stems are found with respect to first and second languages and further happen to be translations of one another (i.e., bilingual stem pairs), then the candidate translation under test is said to be covered with respect to stem. The set of stems for FR and PT are represented as separate keyword trees (Gusfield, 1997) and are learnt by applying the bilingual learning approach (Karimbi Mahesh et al., 2014a) on the FR-PT lexicon of word-to-word translations. Alternatively, existing stemmer may be employed for the purpose. Aho-corasick set-matching algorithm (Gusfield, 1997) is applied to allow faster search over the known stems represented as keyword tree.

As elaborated in Section 4.1, the bilingual suffixes that attach to a bilingual stem are chosen based on their occurrence frequencies in the bilingual suffix list learnt from FR-PT validated lexicon. Hence, naturally, the bilingual pair satisfies the suffix agreement requirement and hence is covered with respect to suffix.

For instance, consider the newly induced correspondences ('délivr', 'emit') and their associated bilingual suffixes, ('er', 'ir'), ('é', 'ido') with surface forms ('délivrer', 'emitir'), ('délivré', 'emitido'). We check if 'délivr' matches the set of stems in FR represented as a keyword tree. If so, we check if 'emit' matches the set of stems in PT. If a match is found in both the languages, we check if ('délivr', 'emit') appears as valid stem pair in the set of bilingual stems learnt from FR-PT validated lexicon. MC_{stm} is set to 0 if the candidate stem pair is found, else is set to 1. For any induced translation, the feature value representing the suffix coverage is set to 0. This is because, for each bilingual stem induced via pivoting, its bilingual extensions are those bilingual suffixes (transitive correspondences) that are observed at least three times in the bilingual suffix list learnt from training dataset for FR-PT.

5   Experimental Setup

5.1   Datasets for Pivoted Induction

The bilingual segments (stems and suffixes) used for pivoted induction were learnt from validated EN-FR and EN-PT bilingual lexicons. The statistics of the bilingual resources for EN-PT and EN-FR used in pivot based lexicon induction is as shown in Table 2. For each of the language pairs listed in first column, the second column shows the count of manually accepted word-to-word translations used in acquiring the bilingual resources comprising of stem pairs and suffix pairs. Similarly, the third, fourth and fifth columns respectively show the statistics of bilingual stems, suffixes and bilingual suffix classes learnt. A suffix class corresponds to set of bilingual suffixes representing bilingual extensions for a set of bilingual stems. It may or may not correspond to Part-of-Speech such as noun, verb, adverb or adjective. However, there are cases where the same suffix class aggregates nouns, adjectives and adverbs.

Table 2: Word-to-word translations for EN-FR and EN-PT with the bilingual stem and suffix statistics

Language Pair	Word-word Tanslations	Bilingual Stems	Bilingual Suffixes	Bilingual Suffix Classes
EN-FR	148,441	18,095	261	77
EN-PT	209,739	24,223	232	136

5.2   Datasets for Classification

In order to train a binary classifier capable of evaluating the newly induced FR-PT bilingual pairs, a total of 162,790 word-to-word bilingual pairs were used as the training dataset. 116,621 accepted word-to-word translations were used as positive examples while 46,169 rejected entries formed the negative examples. The FR-PT training and test datasets used in training and testing the classifier were extracted using the approaches mentioned in the Section 3.

Table 3: Training and test data statistics for FR-PT classifier

Dataset	Accepted	Rejected	Total
Training	116,621	46,169	162,790
Test	6,138	2,430	8,568

5.3 SVM-based Binary Classifier

SVM based tool, LIBSVM[4] was used to learn the binary classifier. Grid-search was performed on RBF kernel parameters (C, γ) using cross-validation to enable accurate predictions for the test data.

Table 4: Performance of the FR-PT word-word classifier on FR-PT test set

Features	P_{Acc}	R_{Acc}	P_{Rej}	R_{Rej}	μ_P	μ_R	μ_F	Accuracy
StrSim	74.38	97.93	73.87	14.77	74.13	56.35	64.03	74.35
StrSim + MC_{stm}	81.10	98.70	92.71	41.89	86.91	70.3	77.73	82.59
StrSim + $MC_{stm+sfx}$	81.96	98.89	94.15	42.02	88.06	71.96	79.20	83.61

The SVM-based FR-PT classifier for word-word translations with a micro average f-measure (Equation 8) approximating 80% (last row of the Table 4) when tested on the test dataset shown in Table 3, trained with the features elaborated in Section 4.3, was used in classifying the newly induced bilingual morph-units. The classifier was trained using the string similarity based features (StrSim), apart from the features regarding stem pairs and suffix pairs. Orthographic similarity measure based on edit distance (Levenshtein, 1966) was used to quantify the similarity between terms on either sides of the bilingual pair (surface form).

6 Evaluation

The evaluation metrics for the classifier and the translation suggestion task are elaborated in the Subsections 6.1 and 6.2 respectively.

6.1 Classification

The classifier results were evaluated with the standard evaluation metrics, Precision (P), Recall (R) and Accuracy, for accepted (Acc) and rejected (Rej) translation pairs, and are computed as given below:

$$P_{Rej} = t_n/(t_n + f_n) \tag{1}$$

$$P_{Acc} = t_p/(t_p + f_p) \tag{2}$$

$$R_{Acc} = t_p/(t_p + f_n) \tag{3}$$

$$R_{Rej} = t_n/(t_n + f_p) \tag{4}$$

$$Accuracy = (t_p + t_n)/(t_p + f_p + t_n + f_n) \tag{5}$$

In the equations 1 through 5, t_p is the number of terms correctly classified as *accepted*, t_n is the number of terms correctly classified as *rejected*, f_p is the number of *incorrect* terms misclassified as *accepted* and f_n is the number of *correct* terms misclassified as *rejected*. P_{Acc} and R_{Acc} denotes precision and recall for the accepted class, and P_{Rej} and R_{Rej} represents precision and recall for the rejected class.

To assess the global performance over both classes, the Micro-average Precision (μ_P), Micro-average Recall (μ_R) and Micro-average f-measure (μ_F) were used, and calculated as shown in equations 6 through 8 below:

$$\mu_P = (P_{Acc} + P_{Rej})/2 \tag{6}$$

---

[4]A library for support vector machines - Software available at http://www.csie.ntu.edu.tw/~cjlin/libsvm

$$\mu_R = (R_{Acc} + R_{Rej})/2 \tag{7}$$

$$\mu_F = 2 * \mu_P * \mu_R/(\mu_P + \mu_R) \tag{8}$$

6.2 Generation

The precision for generated bilingual pairs[5] is calculated as the fraction of correctly generated bilingual pairs to the total number of bilingual pairs generated.

6.2.1 Manual Evaluation

Manual classifications are based on the observations that certain translations are wrong (incomplete or inadequate) (examples labelled as 'Reject' in Table 7). For instance, some of the newly suggested translations are inadequate as they miss an auxiliary verb form in French or a relative pronoun in Portuguese or a negation expression "n'...pas" in French that is also missing in Portuguese ('não'). Despite adjective gender differences in French and Portuguese, no one will be able to know a priori the chosen translation for any noun and the adjective number and gender in French (or in Portuguese) will depend on the chosen French (Portuguese) noun translation.

7 Results and Discussion

As summarised in Table 5, experiments using EN-FR and EN-PT lexicons enabled induction of 28,755 unique transitive bilingual stem correspondences with 1,047 unique bilingual suffix correspondences for FR-PT, contributing to a total of 272,193 unique word-to-word surface translation candidates.

Table 5: Statistics for pivoted bilingual stems, suffixes and translations induced for FR-PT

Description	Bilingual Stems	Bilingual Suffixes	Word-Word Translations
Unique Correspondences	28,755	1,047	272,193

Exclusive automatic validation of newly induced stem pairs using FR-PT binary classifier show that 1,022 candidate bilingual stems matched with the validated and accepted bilingual stems learnt (Karimbi Mahesh et al., 2014a) from the training dataset (word to word translations) for FR-PT. 2,016 stem pairs were orthographically similar (cognates). 19,946 bilingual stem correspondences did not exist in the training data used for classification.

Table 6: Results of classification on FR-PT bilingual morph units

Features	Bilingual Stems
Matching Correspondences (Pivot && Bilingually learnt)	1,022
Orthographically Similar	2,016
Total Correspondences automatically validated	3,038

Evaluation of 126 pivoted FR-PT bilingual suffixes-only show that 108 of them were correct and 21 were incorrect, yielding the precision 84%. Further, manual validation of induced pairs (surface translations) indicates precision approximating 60%.

Among the 272,193 FR-PT inflected word-to-word translations generated via pivoted induction, it was observed that 234,000 were new entries that had not been extracted by any other methods. 38,000 entries had already been extracted by other methods. 39,000 of the new translations generated by pivoted induction (that have not been extracted by any other method) did occur in the parallel corpora, with 13,000 entries co-occurring only once, 7,000 co-occurring twice and 2,000 co-occurring three times.

---

[5] bilingual stems, bilingual suffixes and bilingual surface forms

It is to be noted that the above stated results were achieved using all of the bilingual stems and suffixes learnt from the EN-PT and EN-FR lexicon. The automatically learnt bilingual resources comprising of bilingual stems and suffixes that served as knowledge bases for pivoting FR-PT translations were evaluated indirectly in terms of the generation precision considering new translations (surface forms) suggested. Generation precision (computed as specified in Subsection 6.2) was respectively 90%[6] for EN-PT and 81.55%[7] for EN-FR. As all of the automatically learnt bilingual stems and suffixes were used in our experiments, restricting the knowledge bases used in pivoting to only correct bilingual segments would further improve the results.

7.1 Error Analysis

Some of the French suffixes 'é', 'ée', 'és', 'ées', 'u', 'ue' (and others) were wrongly paired with 'ou', 'aram', 'eu', 'eram', 'iu', 'iram' in PT. Generally, these past participle French forms need an auxiliary verb in French, 'a' or 'ont', to give rise to a form in Portuguese ending in 'ou', 'aram', 'eu', 'eram', 'iu', 'iram' and these correspond to verb forms in English ending in 'ed' that sometimes occur with auxiliary verb forms 'has' or 'have'. Examples include 'a soutenu' (FR) ⇔ 'supported' (EN) ⇔ 'has supported' (EN) ⇔ 'apoiou' (PT) and 'ont suscité' (FR) ⇔ 'provoked' (EN) ⇔ 'have provoked' (EN) ⇔ 'provocaram' (PT). It is the generation of single word form in English that gives rise to those errors. An infinitive in French (as 'soutenir') never translates as a present indicative form, either in subjunctive mood (as 'apoiem') or in indicative mood (as 'apoiam') in Portuguese and requires some extensions both in French (a preposition as 'à', 'de', etc.) and in Portuguese (a relative pronoun as 'que').

Table 7: Manual classifications for newly generated translations using the pivoted induction approach (FR-PT). The columns 'Accept' and 'Reject' show correct and wrong translations respectively. The column 'Corresponding Correct Forms' just illustrates some of the correct translations into Portuguese corresponding to wrong translation inducted from FR-PT

FR-PT		Corresponding Correct Forms
Accept	**Reject**	
soutenir ⇔ apoiarem	soutenir ⇔ apoiam	à soutenir ⇔ que apoiam
soutenir ⇔ apoiar	soutenir ⇔ apoiem	de soutenir ⇔ que apoiem
soutenu ⇔ apoiado	soutenu ⇔ apoiou	a soutenu ⇔ apoiou
soutenue ⇔ apoiado	soutenue ⇔ apoiou	este soutenue ⇔ apoiou-se
suscité ⇔ provocado	suscité ⇔ provocaram	ont suscité ⇔ provocaram
suscitées ⇔ provocados	suscité ⇔ provocou	a suscité ⇔ provocou
suscitées ⇔ provocadas	suscitées ⇔ provocaram	ont été suscitées ⇔ provocaram-se
adaptant ⇔ adaptarem	adaptant ⇔ adaptem	adaptant ⇔ que adaptem
adaptant ⇔ adaptando	adaptant ⇔ adaptem	n'adaptant pas ⇔ que não adaptem

In what regards suffixes 'é', 'ée', 'és', 'ées', when auxiliary verb in French is 'est' or 'sont' we have a passive form that generally translates as a passive form in English, while in Portuguese it requires either an auxiliary verb form, as 'é' or 'são', or requires a passive clitic 'se'. Even French may use the clitic 'se' or 's' and auxiliary verb 'être' ('ést' and 'sont'), or the clitic 'on' and auxiliary 'a' or 'ont' (for singular and plural). Suffixes 'é', 'ée', 'és', 'ées' in French belong to a verbal group ending in 'er', as is the case of 'susciter'.

---

[6]Precision shown corresponds to 2,334 evaluated EN-PT surface forms out of a total of 14,530 pairs generated, where 2,283 were correct and 20 were incorrect

[7]Among the evaluated 4254 entries, out of a total of 18,095 EN-FR bilingual pairs generated, 3469 were correct and 785 were incorrect.

8   Conclusion

In this paper, we have explored the possibility of inducing a bilingual lexicon for the language pair FR-PT by learning transitive correspondences between bilingual stems and suffixes for the language pair EN-FR and EN-PT. Unlike the traditional induction scheme using surface translation forms, we used resources comprising of bilingual stems and suffixes as basis for the pivoted induction. Our approach relies on initially learning suffixes and suffixation operations from validated bilingual lexicons of word-to-word translations using a bilingual learning framework. The bilingual segments thus learnt are then utilised in suggesting new translations using pivoted induction strategy.

Newly induced pairs were validated using an SVM-based binary classifier trained on morphological and similarity based features learnt from validated FR-PT bilingual translation lexicon. Manual validation of the induced surface forms shows precision approximating 60%. The results may be improved by using only those bilingual segments that have been classified as 'accepted'. As future work, we intend to experiment with other language pairs such as EN-PT and EN-HI, EN-LT and EN-PT. Experiments on pivoted induction with morphologically rich language as pivot needs to examined. The bilingual morph-units may enable compact representation of bilingual lexicon, apart from their applicability in inducing surface inflected forms.

Acknowledgements

K. M. Kavitha and Luís Gomes acknowledge the Research Fellowship by FCT/MCTES with Ref. nos., SFRH/BD/64371/2009 and SFRH/BD/65059/2009, respectively. This work was further supported by the funded research project ISTRION (Ref. PTDC/EIA-EIA/114521/2009), NOVA LINCS (ref. UID/CEC/04516/2013), FCT-UNL and ISTRION BOX - Translation & Revision, Lda..

References

Judit Ács. 2014. Pivot-based multilingual dictionary building using wiktionary. In *LREC*, pages 1938–1942. ELRA.

José Aires, José Gabriel Pereira Lopes, and Luís Gomes. 2009. Phrase translation extraction from aligned parallel corpora using suffix arrays and related structures. In *Progress in Artificial Intelligence*, pages 587–597. Springer.

Peter F Brown, Vincent J Della Pietra, Stephen A Della Pietra, and Robert L Mercer. 1993. The mathematics of statistical machine translation: Parameter estimation. *Computational linguistics*, 19(2):263–311.

Jorge Costa, Luís Gomes, Gabriel Pereira Lopes, and Luís MS Russo. 2015. Improving bilingual search performance using compact full-text indices. In *International Conference on Intelligent Text Processing and Computational Linguistics*, pages 582–595. Springer.

Luís Gomes and José Gabriel Pereira Lopes. 2011. Measuring Spelling Similarity for Cognate Identification. In *Progress in Artificial Intelligence — 15th Portuguese Conference on Artificial Intelligence, EPIA 2011*, pages 624–633, Lisbon, Portugal, October. Springer.

Luís Gomes. 2009. Parallel texts alignment. Master's thesis, Faculdade de Ciências e Tecnologia da Universidade Nova de Lisboa (FCT-UNL), Monte da Caparica.

Dan Gusfield. 1997. *Algorithms on strings, trees, and sequences: computer science and computational biology.* Cambridge Univ Pr. pages 52–61.

Hiroyuki Kaji and Dashtseren Erdenebat. 2008. Automatic construction of a japanese-chinese dictionary via english. In *LREC*, pages 699–706.

Kavitha Karimbi Mahesh, Luís Gomes, and José Gabriel Pereira Lopes. 2014a. Identification of bilingual segments for translation generation. In *Advances in Intelligent Data Analysis XIII*, volume 8819 of *LNCS*, pages 167–178. Springer International Publishing.

Kavitha Karimbi Mahesh, Luís Gomes, and José Gabriel Pereira Lopes. 2014b. Identification of bilingual suffix classes for classification and translation generation. In *Advances in Artificial Intelligence, IBERAMIA 2014*, LNCS, pages 154–166. Springer.

Adrien Lardilleux and Yves Lepage. 2009. Sampling-based multilingual alignment. In *Proceedings of Recent Advances in Natural Language Processing*, pages 214–218.

Vladimir Iosifovich Levenshtein. 1966. Binary codes capable of correcting deletions, insertions, and reversals. In *Soviet Physics Doklady*, volume 10, pages 707–710.

Luka Nerima and Eric Wehrli. 2008. Generating bilingual dictionaries by transitivity. In *LREC*.

Kyonghee Paik, Satoshi Shirai, and Hiromi Nakaiwa. 2004. Automatic construction of a transfer dictionary considering directionality. In *Proceedings of the Workshop on Multilingual Linguistic Ressources*, pages 31–38. Association for Computational Linguistics.

Xabier Saralegi, Iker Manterola, and Iñaki San Vicente. 2011. Analyzing methods for improving precision of pivot based bilingual dictionaries. In *Proceedings of the Conference on Empirical Methods in Natural Language Processing*, EMNLP '11, pages 846–856, Stroudsburg, PA, USA. Association for Computational Linguistics.

Xabier Saralegi, Iker Manterola, and Iñaki San Vicente. 2012. Building a basque-chinese dictionary by using english as pivot. In *LREC*, pages 1443–1447.

Daphna Shezaf and Ari Rappoport. 2010. Bilingual lexicon generation using non-aligned signatures. In *Proceedings of the 48th annual meeting of the association for computational linguistics*, pages 98–107. Association for Computational Linguistics.

Kumiko Tanaka and Kyoji Umemura. 1994. Construction of a bilingual dictionary intermediated by a third language. In *Proceedings of the 15th Conference on Computational Linguistics - Volume 1*, COLING '94, pages 297–303, Stroudsburg, PA, USA. Association for Computational Linguistics.

Mairidan Wushouer, Tomoyuki Ishida, and Donghui Lin. 2013. A heuristic framework for pivot-based bilingual dictionary induction. In *Culture and Computing (Culture Computing), 2013 International Conference on*, pages 111–116. IEEE.

Mairidan Wushouer, Toru Ishida, Donghui Lin, and Katsutoshi Hirayama. 2014a. Bilingual dictionary induction as an optimization problem. In *Proceedings of the Ninth International Conference on Language Resources and Evaluation, LREC 2014, Reykjavik, Iceland, May 26-31, 2014.*, pages 2122–2129.

Mairidan Wushouer, Donghui Lin, Toru Ishida, and Katsutoshi Hirayama. 2014b. Pivot-based bilingual dictionary extraction from multiple dictionary resources. In *PRICAI 2014: Trends in Artificial Intelligence*, pages 221–234. Springer.

Author Index

Association for Computational Linguistics
209 N. Eighth Street
Stroudsburg, Pennsylvania 18360

ISBN 978-1-5108-3325-8